A Brief Introduction to Social Work Theory

A Brief
Introduction
to Social Work Theory

David Howe

palgrave
macmillan

First published 2009 by
PALGRAVE MACMILLAN

Palgrave Macmillan in the UK is an imprint of Macmillan Publishers Limited, registered in England, company number 785998, of Houndmills, Basingstoke, Hampshire RG21 6XS.

Palgrave Macmillan in the US is a division of St Martin's Press LLC, 175 Fifth Avenue, New York, NY 10010.

Palgrave Macmillan is the global academic imprint of the above companies and has companies and representatives throughout the world.

Palgrave® and Macmillan® are registered trademarks in the United States, the United Kingdom, Europe and other countries

ISBN-13: 978–0–230–23312–6
ISBN-10: 0–230–23312–0

This book is printed on paper suitable for recycling and made from fully managed and sustained forest sources. Logging, pulping and manufacturing processes are expected to conform to the environmental regulations of the country of origin.

A catalogue record for this book is available from the British Library.

A catalog record for this book is available from the Library of Congress.

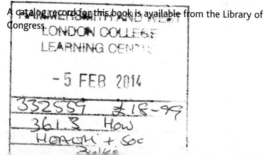

Contents

Acknowledgements

I should like to thank the three anonymous reviewers of the original typescript for their thoughts, suggestions and recommendations. It is always salutary, if not a little humbling to have your efforts exposed to colleagues who immediately see what you're up to and then give you excellent advice about how the whole thing might be improved and better done. On the whole I've tried to follow their advice, although limitations of time, space and ability meant that this was not always possible. Catherine Gray, Palgrave Macmillan's social science publisher and editor, also sees through me and says the most irritatingly sensible things that I wished that I had thought of first. Catherine, thanks for all the sharp editing and overall support. Of course, any weaknesses and imperfections are probably there because I wilfully ignored all the wisdom so generously offered. The failings therefore remain my responsibility.

David Howe
Norwich

1
Social Work Theory

The view from above

If, on the 21 November 1783, you were standing on a small hill just above the river Seine in Paris, not far from where the Eiffel Tower now stands, you would be looking up into the sky. Rising slowly above you is the world's first manned flight and it's in a hot air balloon.

Suspended beneath the open neck at the base of the bright blue and gold balloon, known as a Montgolfier after its maker, is a circular deck. On one side is Pilâtre de Rozier, and on the other, to balance his weight, is the Marquis d'Arlandes. Between them is a brazier that burns straw. The balloon reaches a height of 900 feet and drifts over Paris for 27 minutes. The watching crowds are rapturous. The world is astonished.

In his exquisite book on the science of this age, Richard Holmes (2008) goes on to describe the growing number of balloon flights that took place over the next two decades, both in France and Britain. Some continued to rely on hot air. Others were filled with the recently discovered, very buoyant gas hydrogen. The balloon launches attracted excited crowds of tens of thousands. Within 20 years, the most intrepid balloonists were reaching unbelievable heights of 10,000 feet or more, drifting for miles, and even crossing the English Channel.

But amazing as these feats of flying were, they also delivered an unexpected prize. Rising above the busy cities and countryside, these 'aerial travellers' saw the world in a new, completely different way. As they ascended, the seemingly random bustle and tangle of towns, fields and forest began to take on shape. Patterns and order started to appear. In the silent air above the land, reason and logic could be discerned in the doings of men and women – in the design of streets, the direction of roads, the layout of meadows, the siting of towns and villages. There were also rhythms to be seen between land and sea, rivers and mountains, valleys and hills.

This was the beginning of the Age of Wonder (Holmes 2008). Between 1770 and 1830 science began to get into its full stride. Rising above the world, both literally and metaphorically, men and women began to make sense of the buzz and confusion of everyday life and events. And in the broadest possible way, making sense is what theories help us to do. They rise above the detail and help us to find regularities, patterns and order in what we see and do. They look for relationships between one thing and another.

Ways of knowing

The idea of looking for order and making sense is of great help to all those who have to grapple with the everyday world, not just of nature but also of people. The world of people, of course, is social work's domain.

The more the world makes sense or feels meaningful, the easier it is to negotiate our way around it. If the world in which we work happens to be complicated and turbulent, the need to make sense and know our way around it is even more urgent. Social workers practice in such a world. They deal with people in need and under stress. They operate in environments where there is inequality and injustice. Power, money and opportunities are not fairly distributed.

All of these are tricky matters with which to deal. If social workers are to be sharp and responsive, they simply have to try and make sense and find meaning. Otherwise, the people and situations they work with remain a puzzle. Not being able to understand what's going on is stressful, both for the worker and the client.

Very loosely then, theories are particular ways of making sense. They help social workers see regularities and familiar patterns in the muddle of practice. By stepping back and rising above the hubbub, they help us see what's going on.

Beckett (2006: 33) defines theory in social work as 'a set of ideas or principles to guide practice'. If you can make sense of what is going on, then you're half way towards knowing what to do. There is a good case for having an even more relaxed view of theories by simply calling them 'ways of knowing' (Fook 2002: 68).

This makes theories and ways of knowing very practical things to have under your belt and in your head. The theoretically informed social worker remains steady in the midst of confusion, curious about the unexplained, caring in the face of distress, and compassionate in the presence of need. Social work theories are therefore good things to have if you want your practice to be sensitive, intelligent and organized. Susser puts all of this much more poetically:

> ... to practice without theory is to sail an uncharted sea; theory without practice is not to set sail at all. (Susser 1968, quoted in Hardiker and Barker 1991: 87)

There is no doubt that service users appreciate and respond well to social workers who want to understand, make sense and find meaning. Service users, says Payne (2002: 136), 'are entitled to know that *we have an organized view of what we are doing and why* and gain understanding and explanation of what we are doing, so that they can agree or disagree with it' (emphasis added). 'Organized views' are what theories give us.

Why are there so many social work theories?

You will see from the contents page of this book that there are rather a lot of theories in social work. If theories are attempts to find order and make sense of reality, why do the psychosocial sciences in general and social work in particular have so many? More worryingly perhaps, why do so many of psychosocial sciences' theories clash, disagree, argue and dismiss one another? The answer seems to lie in the fundamental differences to be found in the character of the natural world of things on the one hand, and the social world of people on the other.

As we have seen, theory generation represents the attempt by men and women to explain reality, including physical, psychological and social reality. Some theories are more abstract and high level than others. Newton's theory of gravity and laws of motion are supported by mathematical formulae that allow an extraordinary level of accuracy to be achieved in predicting the motion of stars, planets and satellites. They are essential when it comes to landing men and women on the moon and guiding spacecraft to exactly the right spot on the planet Mars.

Social and psychological theories do not have this degree of exactness. If people are not like objects, then it is unlikely that social and psychological theories can ever be quite like the natural sciences. Rocks, atoms and light beams in themselves are meaningless. In contrast human beings are full of meaning. We have ideas about ourselves, who we are and what we are about. We are self-defining as well as socially defined.

Our psychological development takes place as we relate and interact with others, as we negotiate and create meaning for ourselves and others. The social and psychological sciences therefore have to deal with subjective experience as well as objective reality – what people think, feel, and believe as well as what they say and do. This is why language and the quality of the relationship are so important in the conduct of social work.

Language mediates so much of our experience. We try to make sense of ourselves, other people, culture and the world in general using language. We try to understand and be understood using words. The meaning that we give to our own and other people's experience is therefore language dependent.

But language is slippery. It's open to interpretation, misunderstanding and misuse. It changes over time. It is never fixed. It differs between countries and cultures.

So if meaning is carried by language and language is never still, never stable, never exact, it is not possible to capture personal meaning and social experience in the way that the natural sciences fix physical reality. This is why the social sciences and the humanities can never be quite like the natural sciences. They explore personal experience as well as external behaviour.

Personal experience and social reality are therefore socially constructed (Berger and Luckmann 1971). This means that there are many social theories each seeking to make sense of human behaviour and social life. Society being socially constructed means that it is 'a fluid, precarious, negotiated field of loosely connected activities. It is held together, ultimately, by the thin threads of shared understandings and a common language' (Seidman 2004: 82).

It is therefore inevitable that social work, which is an applied psychosocial science, will also be rich, varied and contested. The psychosocial sciences have developed a dizzying array of ideas to fathom the individual, the relationship, the family, the group, and the community as well as the cultures and societies in which they all live. Social work and its theories reflect this richness, which, after all, reflects the richness of the human experience. We also see this extraordinary diversity of interest reflected in the ways in which social work has been defined.

For example, social workers, according to Beckett (2006: 4), work with people 'who are in some way vulnerable, excluded or disadvantaged in society'. He continues that it is the job of social workers to help people meet their needs, improve their circumstances and reach their potential. The business of social work is therefore something to do with enhancing personal wellbeing. The International Association of Schools of Social Work and Federation of Social Workers (2001) add that wellbeing is also achieved by promoting freedom, personal power, social change, and problem-solving in personal relationships.

Back on the ground, all of this social work concern and action take place at the point where individuals, families, groups and society brush up against each other.

Three quick examples make the point. Family and neighbours begin to worry whether 86-year-old Mary can continue looking after herself at home, although she feels quite happy where she is. The hospital has a concern that the injuries suffered by a 2-year-old boy may not be accidental. The police are called to the local shopping mall to attend to a young man with mental health problems who is shouting abuse at passers-by.

These relatively straightforward, everyday concerns are packed with political issues and moral dilemmas. There are issues of freedom and equality, order and conflict. And although these examples may be unexceptional, they demand some working knowledge of an extraordinary range of academic disciplines.

Add to these examples the interest that many social workers have in matters of human rights and social justice, and it soon becomes apparent that if good practice is driven by sound knowledge, then social workers need to know an awful lot of very different things. Even in the simplest of cases, there's usually much to think about. To practise well, social workers have to think well, and to think well, they have to know a good deal.

Putting it rather grandly, social workers engage with the human condition. If they are to work competently with people in need and distress it is inevitable that social workers will need to know something of the many disciplines that have tried to make sense of human experience. This is likely to include psychology and sociology, political theory and philosophy, social policy and cultural studies, communications theory and organizational behaviour, the law and criminology. Little wonder that social work's key introductory textbooks are long and weighty. They have to be.

So, in contrast, what can be made of a book that claims to be brief, introductory and about social work theory?

The aim here is not to be comprehensive. Nor can this book attempt to be definitive. Instead, the hope is that the reader will gain a sense of why social work finds itself so involved and interested in so many types of knowledge.

Reasons for choosing a particular social work theory

It will also be apparent that in order to survive and develop some professional expertise, not everything can be known. Indeed, only some things can be known well. Quite what these things will be is likely to depend on the individual social worker's moral sympathies, intellectual inclinations and emotional character.

Matters are made even more challenging when the social worker is faced with not only a vast range of books on this theory or that practice, but also with the authors of these books who are nearly always passionate and persuasive about the critical importance of their approach and their understanding of social work.

I'm not the most critical of readers. I am easily won over by an enthusiastic writer or a committed advocate of one approach or another. Although this might seem weak minded, I prefer to see it as a recognition that people and society are rather complex matters, particularly when they interact. Each theory, each approach is saying something interesting about human nature and social life. Further reflection might make you more cautious and less convinced of this idea or that model, but there might be an element of truth in most, if not all theories.

So how to choose? Well, closer examination of one's own beliefs and convictions might rule out some approaches while ruling in others. The perceived merits and conceptual rigour of one particular theory might appeal to the intellect. Or the idea that social work should be like medicine and base its practice on methodologically sound research about what works might sound eminently sensible. Or the way another theory celebrates our shared humanity might convince us morally and so win the day.

Being brief, this introduction to social work theory aims to give you a feel for the subject. Inevitably there will be bias in what I say and choose to emphasize. Often the bias will be implicit, but sometimes I'll come clean.

The idea is not to get you to agree or become an expert. Rather, the hope is that you will become intrigued by the way different thinkers have tried to make sense of people and society. You are then free to pursue their thoughts in more detail. To the extent that social work applies sociology, psychology and political theory, our subject matter should excite the intellect. After all, people and what they think, feel, and do is our business.

Certainly, many would-be practitioners are motivated to consider a career in social work because of a strong interest in people. Many also feel great concern about the inequalities and injustices suffered by society's more vulnerable and disadvantaged groups. There is a wish to make their lot better. But whatever the drive, many of these feelings boil down to a simple wish to help people.

Easily dismissed as naïve, the idea of wanting to help people in need has an honourable pedigree. Bill Jordan, in a compelling personal account, wrote a classic text with the title *Helping in Social Work*. In his book, Jordan (1979: 26) values social workers who are truthful, who ring true, who help people feel better by listening, who 'recognize' their fellow men and women and treat them as valued and 'real'. Behind the ability to be sincere and authentic lies a genuine interest in people driven by an unquenched curiosity about what makes each and every one of us tick, and what helps us live together in the good society.

Wondering why

The best way to get into a theoretical way of thinking about what you do and how you do it is to ask the question 'why?' People who are curious and want to know what's going on tend to be interested in ideas, theories and explanations. It is my hope that this book will excite your curiosity.

So, why do people do the things they do? Why is there social inequality and injustice? Why does a father get so angry and violent? Why does a depressed woman feel so anxious and sad? How does stress affect people?

Asking 'why?' questions is generally a good thing to do if you want your practice to be considered, thoughtful and justified. Intellectual curiosity is likely to keep us professionally alive and alert. As we have seen, theories are particularly good things to have if we want answers to these practice questions. They help us to understand what might be going on. Coulshed and Orme agree:

> Social workers, to be truly effective, need to be constantly asking 'why?' It is in this quest for understandings about, for example, why situations arise, why people react in certain ways and why particular interventions might be utilized, that theory informs practice. (2006: 9)

Moreover, the more we are aware of the many different ways we can think about a person, a need or a problem, the more humble and less dogmatic we are likely to be, and that, say Hardiker and Barker (1991: 97), is no bad thing for a social worker.

The plan of this book is to keep the flame of curiosity burning by wandering, indeed wondering across social work's bumpy, complicated but never dull terrain. We shall not stay too long with each theory but move briskly on to gain a sense of how different social work ideas view people and their social situations. The aim is to gain a feel for the kinds of practice that each theoretical approach inspires.

It will also become apparent as we explore social work's practices that theoretical fashions change. This alerts us to the idea that what we know and think as social workers is embedded in the bigger political picture. Social work finds itself being swept along by the grand themes of history. Particular theories and practices bob up at certain times and in particular places.

Occasionally, a particular theory will dominate a decade only to fade into the professional background. We shall try and appreciate the theories and their practices and the broad social movements that toss them to prominence before the tide of history drops them and moves on. However, few of social work's theories and practices ever entirely disappear. They wash through social work, leaving behind traces of their ideas and thoughts. It is as if each theory discovers a particular insight into our shared fate and so we are reluctant to let it go.

But before we get too involved with the fates of different theories, let's go back to the beginning and explore social work's origins.

2
Origins

Hard times

Although the kind of things that social workers do – helping people in distress, trying to improve the resources of those in need, keeping the vulnerable safe – have been done as far back as anyone can remember, it is generally acknowledged that social work as a recognized practice began to take shape in the nineteenth century.

In the West this was a time of rapid industrialization. People were leaving their small rural communities in vast numbers and being drawn into the fast growing cities to work in factories. Rural poverty was the main driving force. But when families reached the cities, many suffered low wages, poor housing, overcrowding, disease and stress. Poverty and misery continued to be the lot of these new working classes.

However, although wages and conditions might have been no better in the countryside, at least there was a tradition of small community support. Extended families might help care for an ageing relative or cousin with a learning difficulty. The move to the growing industrial cities meant that family life fragmented. There were no established communities in the big towns to offer help and support at times of need. There was no state help or benefits as we know them today. If you fell into poverty or found yourself sick, old and alone, or out of work and disabled, the only options were to beg, starve, rely on charity, go into the workhouse or die.

These were tough and turbulent times. Old orders were breaking down. Crime was rife. The problem of drink among the urban poor was common. And many felt that the squalor and overcrowding of the industrial cities was a breeding ground for vice and wickedness.

There was certainly a growing fear among the privileged classes that social disorder was on the increase. The aristocracy, the land-rich and the middle classes began to fear that such misery could lead to social unrest, anger and maybe even revolution. 'It is unsafe to have amongst us,' said one 1867 report, 'an ever-increasing number of starving, desperate men' (quoted in Woodruffe 1962: 49). Questions began to be asked about the nature of the huge social changes that were taking place. Worries were expressed about the possible causes of the growing problem of unruly behaviour among the very poor. Politicians and social thinkers wanted answers.

Science and social science

The industrial revolution had both fed off and fed into the success of the natural sciences. The power of human reason was beginning to fathom the world of nature. Nature slowly began to reveal her secrets and the laws that underpinned them. This was the Age of Enlightenment.

Out of what was previously called 'natural philosophy' emerged the modern natural sciences; chemistry, physics, biology, geology. Nature was slowly being explained by science. And once explained, nature could be controlled, changed, harnessed and exploited. The natural world was gradually falling under the control of men and women. The Scientific Revolution was ushering in the Industrial Revolution. However, there was a price being paid. Material success was being achieved at the cost of great social pain and personal failure.

So what to do about the growing problem of the increasingly impoverished working classes? Well, if human reason could tame and exploit nature, then it seemed logical to apply the same human talent to solving the problems of society. While the natural sciences were studying and explaining the material world, the newly minted social sciences could do the same job on people and the social world; explain them, order them, control them and improve them.

Was it possible, though, to study human nature and society scientifically? Could people's behaviour be analysed and the problems of how best to live together be answered? The scale of the social and behavioural changes that were taking place in the late eighteenth and nineteenth centuries gave a major impetus to answering these questions. And it was out of these social enquiries that the new disciplines of psychology, sociology and economics emerged. The time also saw the birth of the modern state.

The modern state seeks order. It has an idea of how people should behave. Discussing the ideas of Zygmunt Bauman (1992), Seidman explains that the state:

> aspires not merely to rule, protect its citizens, or ensure prosperity, but to tame and domesticate the disorder of human desire. The modern state is inconceivable without intellectuals. To run the bureaucratic apparatus of modernity requires information about the dynamics of populations, institutions, and whole societies. Expert knowledges are required for the management of schools, factories, welfare institutions, prisons, hospitals, and local and national governments ... The modern state and Enlightenment social science emerged simultaneously and exhibit an affinity of interest and spirit. (Seidman 2004: 194–5)

In studying these new social sciences, it was always the plan not only to understand society but to change it, to apply the knowledge created to the problems of society. Social scientific knowledge, it was agreed, could, and should help promote social progress and a better society. And one of the practices to emerge out of the idea of applying the social sciences to real world concerns was social work (see Seed 1973 and Payne 2005b for good introductions to the history of social work).

Social work looked to sociology to explain how the problems of the poor were really problems of social structure. Sociological analyses encouraged social reform and taking social action.

Social work was also being influenced by psychology which was beginning to explain the behaviour of people, particularly those who had problems and those who were problems. Psychological analyses encouraged changing the individual. They valued treatment and therapy.

It is possible, even at this very early stage, to see a parting of the social work ways. Applied sociology suggested social action and political reform. Applied psychology was seeking ways to help the individual function better and be a productive, trouble-free member of society. These tensions and splits in social work's theoretical make-up – between social reform and individual change – are still present today.

Social science and the humanities

However, the growth of the psychosocial sciences and their application did not mean the end of social work's long-standing commitment to its values. Care of the poor, and concern for the weak have
always been defining features of social work. For many practitioners,
the caring relationship between one human being and another had
always been at the heart of sound practice. From social work's beginnings, the knowledge sought to support relationship-based practices
has tended to come from the arts and humanities, moral philosophy and religious values rather than from the social sciences.
Relationship-based social work is not necessarily hostile to science,
but it believes that experience rather than experiment underpins our
shared humanity.

It is here that we glimpse yet another parting of the theoretical
ways – social work based on the psychosocial sciences, and social
work inspired by the arts and humanities. The split between the two
cultures of science and art runs deep in our society. In 1956, C. P.
Snow wrote an article in which he regretted this division. His aim was
to unite the two worlds.

Snow's thesis was that the failure of the arts to understand science,
and science to appreciate the arts was to the detriment of both. If we
are fully to grasp the nature of human experience, we need to understand ourselves biologically and psychologically, sociologically and
politically, experientially and spiritually, existentially and interpersonally, artistically and creatively. Social work has explored all of
these types of knowledge and experience in its attempt to connect
with, understand and help people with problems and people who are
problems. Nevertheless, social work continues to straddle the two
cultures with some discomfort.

It is almost as if temperamentally there are two types of social
worker. There is the practitioner who longs for clarity and certainty.
Her appeal is to the rigour of scientific thought and analysis.
Observation and measurement bring her objective knowledge. The
demand is that social workers provide evidence for the effectiveness
of what they do. If practice is not evidence-based, then on what possible ethical grounds can social workers justify what they do? The
only way to get evidence is to carry out scientific research that trials
and tests practices and their outcomes.

In contrast, there are practitioners who believe that people and relationships are far too complex, too subtle fully to be captured by the necessarily simple, even one-dimensional approaches of the applied sciences. It is being in the relationship itself that gives the social worker and service user insight into, and experience of what is truly going on. It is only by subjectively appreciating the other person's experience that understanding and knowledge are achieved. Humanistic philosophies, novels, poetry and art can give us great insight into these processes. Effective practice occurs when practitioners share their humanity with service users.

We shall see that social work theory and its practice have not developed in a straight historical line. Our journey through the ideas that have helped shaped the profession will twist and turn, but wherever we go, we find ourselves treading in the footsteps, albeit some distance behind, of the many great minds that have pondered the nature of society and the human condition.

3
Casework and Social Reform

Charitable works

As we have seen, the energy of Victorian Britain was making the country very rich. And yet amid such wealth, millions were poor and getting poorer. Death through starvation was not uncommon.

There was a belief held by many that it was hard work that led to success and wealth. The argument went that people who were poor found themselves in a parlous state simply because they were idle. Idleness was a sin, and to be sinful was to be ungodly. The proper aim of Christian charity therefore was to help the poor return to God and to work. The offer of material and financial support carried the danger of demoralizing the recipient, sapping his fibre and resolve to work, encouraging dependency and fecklessness.

However, it was gradually becoming apparent to more thoughtful observers that the existence of so much misery, hunger and hardship could hardly be blamed on the poor themselves. It seemed increasingly clear that so much destitution and desperation was the result of economic, social and structural problems and not laziness.

Disraeli talked of Britain's 'Two Nations'. Charles Dickens' novels were already painting terrible pictures of the desperate lives being lived by so many while the greedy, selfish few lived in great luxury and ignorance.

The enquiries of journalists and philanthropists began to reveal the extent and depth of the sheer awfulness of what it was like to be poor, not just in the great industrial cities but in the hidden villages and hamlets of rural Britain. Charles Booth carried out a series of major surveys into the miserable lives and chronic want of London's poor. Government Reports were commissioned. And so slowly 'the Victorian conscience was stabbed into action' (Woodruffe 1962: 8).

Of course, philanthropists, voluntary workers and charities had always played a part in responding to the needs of the sick, orphaned, homeless, old and poor. This became increasingly true as Britain moved into the nineteenth century. So although the vast scale of Victorian poverty was overwhelming, there were members of the more privileged classes who were conscience-stricken and moved to action.

Philanthropists are wealthy people who choose to give away some of their money for the public good. In the nineteenth century, some became founders of the great charities. Informing the beliefs of many of those who ran these charities was the idea that social work should be about strengthening people's character. Self-help and self-improvement therefore ran as a leitmotif throughout much of social work's early purpose.

The birth of the caseworker

As the nineteenth century ticked by, more and more charities began to appear – for hospitals and the sick, for guidance of the morally fallen, for support of the injured and unemployed, for orphans and abandoned children. But there was no underlying 'method' to deliver these social work services. There were no criteria to determine who should and should not be helped – who were the 'deserving' and who were the 'undeserving' poor. So much of the help given seemed indiscriminate and uncoordinated.

Finally, in response to this well-meaning but muddled situation, the Charity Organization Society (COS) was founded in 1869. It attempted to streamline, discipline and systematize the work of the hundreds of charities and the social work services they offered. It is in these early efforts of the COS that we find the origins of the social caseworker.

The aim of the COS was to reduce 'pauperism'. This would be achieved by supporting only those in want who were deserving of help, and 'likely to benefit'. Caseworkers would encourage the recipients of their help to develop habits of thriftiness and independence through improved strength of character. Those who did not 'deserve' help were left to the cold embrace of the Poor Law.

These principles of practice were enthusiastically espoused by the hugely influential figure of Charles Stewart Loch who was appointed Secretary of the COS in 1875, a position which he occupied for the next 38 years. He was deeply committed to ridding society of poverty and misery. And this would be achieved, he believed, by helping families stay together, by challenging men and women to be independent and hard-working.

It was believed the family was the unit that was best suited to bring up children, look after the sick and care for older people. In order to determine who deserved help, caseworkers should carry out a thorough investigation of the circumstances and character of those applying for charitable support.

Loch did not accept that social and economic forces had any part to play in the causes of poverty and distress. Failure to achieve 'self-dependence' was a problem of the weakness of the individual's character. He was therefore opposed to State intervention. State organized relief would undermine the grit of the working classes and their resolve to stay employed.

Training to be a caseworker

Although we might bridle at some of the principles proposed by Loch and the COS, many of the basic characteristics of social casework were laid down in these early years. Caseworkers should *investigate* the causes of the problem. This involved a *home visit*, an *interview*, and an investigation or enquiry to establish 'deservingness '. *Written case notes* were kept for *analysis* and *record*.

If these tasks were to be done well, they would require skill, technique and training. People could change, given help and guidance. With support, the individual who had fallen on hard times could be helped to get back on his or her feet. A widower might be given a mangle and trained to take in and iron laundry. The father who had suffered a leg injury might be found a job that didn't require him to stand for long periods. If loans were made, the expectation was that they would be re-paid by instalments. There was dignity in work.

Loch's insistence that his workers should be trained to conduct *purposeful interviews* in order to produce well-formulated *assessments* laid down one of social work's most enduring traditions: individual casework. If Loch's view was that problems and need were caused by the failings at the level of the individual, then the solution lay in helping individuals sort out their problems.

With a focus on the individual and the family, the new science of psychology was likely to offer casework its most useful theoretical base. The scientific method had worked with brilliant success when applied to the natural world. It was expected to work equally well when applied to individuals and their behaviour. 'If we wish to improve the condition of the poor,' said Loch, 'we must adopt the scientific method' (quoted in Woodruffe 1962: 48). For him, if charity work was to be effective, it must be carried out by trained 'social physicians' (*The Charities Register and Digest* 1895: x cited in Woodruffe 1962: 53).

So began social work's long standing interest in applying psychological theories to social work practice. As new theories and explanations of human behaviour were generated by psychologists, so new social work theories and practices arose. Over the past hundred years, social work, as casework, has been excited by psychoanalytic theory, ego psychology, behavioural and cognitive psychology, and humanistic approaches.

As it assimilated these theories into its practices, social work developed its own body of knowledge. The knowledge could be written down in books, pamphlets and papers. It could be stored and catalogued in universities. Once codified, these *professional bodies of knowledge* could be transmitted by teachers from one generation to the next. This allows new workers to be trained in that body of knowledge. Knowledge, formalized training and the award of qualifications are now part and parcel of modern-day professional education, but they had their origins in the late nineteenth and early twentieth centuries (Seed 1973).

Social reform

In the opposite camp to the caseworkers were those nineteenth century reformers who believed that personal problems were really social problems. For them, the answer lay in improving social and economic conditions. This would be achieved by organizing community action, social change and social reform.

The radical tradition therefore wanted social and economic change at the structural level. This reforming tradition argued for state intervention and improved welfare provision. Better housing, education, and social security were the way forward. Social workers need to understand how society and social justice work. Sociology and social policy are the preferred knowledge bases of these reforming approaches. Social group work, community development and political action are the methods of choice.

The settlement movement

The 'Settlement Movement' represented an early version of these more sociologically inspired practices. However, even here, the origins of community-oriented responses lay in the Charity Organization Society.

There were members of the COS who campaigned for the improvement of social conditions. These more socially aware individuals reflected a growing sense among many of the philanthropic classes that the solution for many personal problems probably lay in mobilizing community resources and arguing for social change. And if this was to work, 'educated' volunteers would have to live and settle in the deprived, disadvantaged and 'less educated' communities that were in need of help.

Perhaps best known of these pioneering 'settlement' workers was Canon Samuel Augustus Barnett who was himself inspired by the earlier work of Edward Denison. After graduating from the University of Oxford, Denison went to live in the East End of London specifically to learn about the distressed conditions of the poor and working classes. It soon struck him that charity and almsgiving were not the answer. Rather, what the labouring classes needed was better education, improved justice, and leadership to be provided by those of 'good education'.

Barnett, himself an Oxford graduate, took on the rudiments of Denison's ideas. His appointment as a priest in East London's Whitechapel area brought him face to face with the misery and awfulness of Victorian poverty. In papers delivered at both the Universities of Oxford and Cambridge, Barnett described the terrible conditions of the poor and what might be done about them. Roused by descriptions of such deprivation, the Universities were moved to found and maintain what became known as 'Settlements' in East London. The first, named Toynbee Hall after Barnett's friend, Arnold Toynbee, a brilliant Oxford scholar who died at the young age of 31, appeared in 1884. Barnett was appointed as founding warden.

The basic idea was that men and women of education should live in the same areas as the poor. They would offer leadership, neighbourliness and education. However, for the work of the settlements to be of value, one of the first tasks of the workers was to gain a thorough knowledge of the area – who lived there, what were conditions like, what was needed. In effect, Barnett insisted that a good piece of social research was the first thing to do.

Barnett was a pioneer of what we would now call 'group work'. Groups made up of settlement workers and members of the local community would meet and explore possible solutions to local problems. This emphasis on neighbourhood and group work was in marked contrast to the individual casework practised by the COS. Equality between clients and social workers, inspired by the idea that in the eyes of God all men and women are equal, was valued as a practice principle.

In no time at all, the settlement movement spread to other great cities, initially in Britain, but very soon across Europe and the States. When the settlement idea was picked up by American social workers, its interests widened to include demands for improved sanitation, housing and education, as well as better working conditions for the labouring classes.

As new settlements were founded, they continued to expand and innovate the range of their 'social services'. For example, in Manchester:

> ... settlement work extended into readings to the blind, penny banks, social evenings, poor man's lawyers, clubs for boys, for girls, for cripples and for the casuals from the common lodging houses. (Young and Ashton 1956: 231)

The poor could raise their standard of living by gaining knowledge and know-how. They could enjoy social support and friendship. Some settlements ran play centres, nurseries and child welfare clinics.

Fighting the cause

For their part, the young university students, in their role as settlement workers, would learn about and be aware of what it was like to live in poverty. Their knowledge might inform the reports that sought to describe the squalid conditions in which many of the working classes lived. And when they left the settlements, their experience could be used to good effect when they entered public life. Indeed, over the years many great social reformers began their political lives as settlement workers.

Thus, one of the great achievements of the settlements was to raise awareness of the nature and extent of poverty. In this, the settlement workers fulfilled one of social work's central functions, that of representing the poor to the rich, the powerless to the powerful, and the dangerous to the respectable in order to bring about social change. There were wrongs to be righted. There were causes to be won.

4
Cause and Function

The pursuit of causes

A rather different way of thinking about social work's mixed parentage and fractured identity was offered by Porter Lee as far back as 1929. He was an American social work academic who wrote a feisty paper about social work's dual nature, later expanding it into a book with the title *Social Work as Cause and Function* (1937).

Lee felt that temperamentally social workers were inclined either to *pursue causes* or *carry out functions*. In short, social workers are likely to be radical or conservative in their approach to society and its ills.

Radical social workers are interested in how societies organize themselves to benefit the rich and powerful and to punish the poor and weak. They are outraged when they come across unfairness and inequality, neglect and ignorance. So, when nineteenth century activists discovered the problems of family poverty, the plight of the old and sick, child abandonment and cruelty, they campaigned to do something about them. They fought a *cause*.

The successful pursuit of causes requires sociological understanding and political nous. But perhaps even more than these, causes require zeal, passion, even anger. They might even have glamour.

If, for example, you want to improve the lives of disabled children and adults, you need to see how society disadvantages disabled people with its steps and narrow doors, its meagre benefits and social stigma. You need to recognize the limited opportunities of disabled people to get into the labour market. Established interests aren't going to roll over and change the architecture or open up job markets just for disabled people. Radical practitioners have to shout loud and long about such unfairness and discrimination. A cause is therefore about ridding society of a social evil and establishing a personal good.

Carrying out a function

But let's say the cause is won. There is collective recognition that the situation is unacceptable and something should be done about it.

Once the objective of the cause is reached, said Lee (1937), it can be made permanent only by a combination of policies and statutes, organization and education, bureaucracy and training, good administration and the development of a body of knowledge. At this point, social work becomes a *function* of society. Social workers are there to deal with certain types of human need. Their welfare activities are carried out on behalf of any well-organized and civilized community. Social workers contribute to the smooth running of society. They 'are the maintenance mechanics oiling the interpersonal wheels of the community' (Davies 1985: 28).

Back to our example, having won the cause, let's allow that governments change their legislation so that discrimination on grounds of disability is outlawed. Let's concede they increase resources and provisions for disabled men and women, and create social care workers to advise, guide and support disabled people. In effect, social agencies appear whose *function* is to provide a range of statutory approved services. Social care workers carry out these functions guided by laws, policies and procedures. The workers' knowledge and skill base is technical. 'Social work as function' requires minds that are systematic and steady, considered and calm.

So, today's function was yesterday's cause. When the changes demanded by social reformers are finally accepted by the powers-that-be, new policies and the resources to support them begin to appear. It is at this point that the successful cause becomes a social policy, a function of the state. Agencies and their guidelines represent society's acceptance of the rightness of the cause. What Lee was pointing out was that social work needs two kinds of people – those who champion causes, and professionals who can deliver a well thought-out service. But for each of these types of social work, very different emotions, skills and theories are needed.

Campaigns and consequence

Causes and those who pursue them need only justify themselves by their ardent belief, purpose and faith in the moral rightness of the on working with individuals and families and the methods used were those of social casework.

We shall use Mary Richmond's work as a platform to launch a series of accounts describing many of social work's most established and influential theories and their practice. These will include psychodynamic theory, problem-solving approaches, cognitive and behavioural therapies, and task-centred work.

Mary Richmond was born in 1861. Her parents died while she was still a child and she went to live with her grandmother who was something of a suffragette and a radical. After leaving school at 16, Mary took various clerical and book-keeping jobs until at the age of 28 she was offered a temporary post as assistant treasurer to the Charity Organization of Baltimore.

It was at this point that her energies and talent took wing. She was soon promoted to leading roles in various Charity Organizations. Her rapidly growing knowledge and experience also involved her in helping to train social workers.

It was during her years as a manager, organizer and teacher that she began to conceptualize the business of social work. She constantly strived to understand the relationship between the individual and his environment so that the two could be helped to adjust, one to the other in harmony and mutual benefit. Her aim was to help her clients improve in character and to 'grow in personality.' Under her direction, we see social work beginning to define itself as a profession whose focus of interest is the 'person in relationship to his or her environment'.

The social work process

Richmond wanted to understand how 'help' worked. She wanted to know how people could be helped to change. Gradually, she began to conceptualize a process made up of several stages that a social worker would need to follow if she wanted to be effective.

First, the facts of the case, including the social situation, were gathered. Then, a *social diagnosis* based on the facts and the nature of the problem was formulated. This was followed by a review of the resources available, including the help, support and cooperation of others that might be drawn upon. The help and support of the extended family was seen as particularly valuable. Finally, a treatment anger, overcoming their anxiety, or sustaining a relationship could be understood as problems at the psychological level. It therefore followed that if help was to be effective, psychologically-based treatments would be most appropriate.

With societies getting richer, the problems were seen as ones of psychological adjustment and no longer ones of material need. Certainly many people remained in relative poverty – but why did some take to drink and become alcoholics, why did some parents neglect their children but not others, why did some children commit crimes?

It seemed that social and economic conditions alone couldn't explain why some people but not others got into difficulty. Social workers are faced day-in, day-out with human behaviours that are puzzling, seemingly self-defeating, anti-social, and distressing. Maybe psychology and, more specifically, psychoanalytic psychiatry could provide some of the answers?

All in the mind

In this section, the work of Sigmund Freud, and psychoanalytic and psychodynamic theories, is briefly outlined. The role of the unconscious mind and its affect on human behaviour has been particularly important for these theorists. Psychodynamic approaches assume that behaviour is motivated by mental processes, many of which lie outside our conscious awareness. Behaviour is also a feature of our personality. The way an individual reacts to a situation is believed to be a reflection of his or her personality.

Personality develops over time. In psychoanalytic theory, early life experiences, particularly with parents, are thought to play a big part in personality formation. It is the continuing influence of past experiences that lie outside conscious awareness on our behaviour that broadly defines a psychodynamic approach. Unresolved relationship problems, particularly early on in life including those with parents, can cause psychological problems in the present.

For example, children who have been emotionally neglected or rejected will not have been helped to handle the strong emotional arousals that are part and parcel of growing up. As a result they become emotionally stuck or 'fixated' at early stages of infantile development. Even as adults, their feelings and behaviour will be immature and infantile, particularly at times of stress. The result is that they are prone to be impulsive. Their lives are riddled with dramas and crises – evictions, marriage bust-ups, debt, crime and quarrels.

Emotional conflicts also lead to distress and problem behaviours. Like toddlers, adults stuck at emotionally infantile levels will 'act-out' their feelings rather than 'think them through'. Workers therefore have to think what their client's behaviour 'means'. What does this behaviour indicate and say about the client's emotional needs and anxieties?

A mother who insists on spending lots of money on expensive 'treats' because she feels depressed, even though she has major debts, may be telling us something about her own emotionally deprived childhood. She craves love, but doesn't trust it. She is impatient. When she wants something, she wants it now. As a result the house is full of impulsive, comforting foods, toys and gadgets – bars of chocolate, cuddly dolls, a foot massage – even though the rent hasn't been paid for weeks. It was Freud who was one of the first to explore how early childhood experiences could affect adult mental life.

Freud and psychoanalytic theory

Sigmund Freud was born in 1856 in Freiberg, Moravia, now part of the Czech Republic. He went to medical school in Vienna. He began to specialize in the 'neurological disorders' expressed as various mental health problems. His ideas about people's behaviour and mental health gradually took shape and towards the end of the nineteenth century until his death in London in 1939 he fashioned what we now know as psychoanalysis.

Psychoanalysis assumes that the cause of any behaviour is to be found in the mind (the Greek for which is *psyche*, hence psycho-analysis). In-tune with the Darwinian biology of his times, Freud felt that human motivation was governed by *innate drives*. Mental energy flows around a person's mind in a *dynamic*, active fashion generating and affecting thoughts, feelings and behaviours. This is why broader definitions of this approach are sometimes referred to as *psychodynamic* theory.

Freud's ideas evolved and changed over his lifetime. They have greatly influenced not only psychology, psychotherapy and social work, but also literature and the arts. However, I shall offer a stripped down version of psychoanalytic theory for social workers. Some key ideas will be left out. There will be no formal mention of Freud's psychosexual stages of development (oral, anal and phallic), the oedipal complex, or dreams.

What I do want to emphasize are those elements of the theory that have endured and continue to resonate with social workers and their practice. In particular, I want to touch on the origins of anxiety and guilt, resistance, the defence mechanisms, and transference and counter-transference. For anyone interested in relationships and how they work, these ideas continue to fascinate and inform.

The behaviour of many social work clients suggests their minds are not at rest. In some, anxiety leads to a range of mental health problems. In others, anger and aggression get them into behavioural difficulty. For those who are anxious or angry, relationships rarely run smoothly. They have violent rows with partners. Their children are either neglected or abused. Social workers are scorned, anxiously needed, or avoided. There is either over-dependence on a health professional, or a drug, or a drink. A social worker wonders why this client seems always to be his own worst enemy, or why a client hates her so much when she's only trying to help (Brearley 2007: 86). Psychoanalytic and psychodynamic theories seek to cast their own particular lights on these problems and needs.

Talking cures

Freud was a clinician. His clinical experiences with patients were the source of his extraordinary ideas. Influenced by the work of Josef Breuer, Freud began to base his treatments on getting patients to talk about their problems and the thoughts and feelings that underpinned them. Thus, the idea of a therapeutic relationship was born – talking about your worries with another person was itself a help. The therapeutic relationship continues to play a central role in the practice of many social workers.

The story is recounted of Breuer's treatment of a young woman, Anna O (Breuer and Freud 1895/2004; Joseph 2001: 62). She suffered a number of physical symptoms, possibly caused by some previous psychological trauma. During treatment Anna would occasionally express strong feelings. Both Breuer and Anna noticed that the symptoms seemed to disappear as she spoke about her disruptive emotions.

Anna called the treatment her 'talking cure'. It seemed to Breuer, and later Freud, that giving people the opportunity to think aloud and to connect with their feelings in the context of a safe relationship helped them gain *insight* into the possible origins and causes of their anxieties and problems. The opportunity to talk and reflect appeared to be therapeutic. Here lay the beginnings of psychotherapy.

In a review of psychoanalysis, the 'talking cures' and their relationship to literature, Appignanesi (2008: 4) quotes from Virginia Woolf's notes on writing her novel *To The Lighthouse*:

> I wrote my book very quickly; and when it was written, I ceased to be obsessed with my mother. I no longer heard her voice; I do not see her. I suppose I did for myself what psychoanalysts do for their patients. I expressed some very long felt and deeply felt emotion. And in expressing it I explained it and then laid it to rest ...

The value of giving people the chance to talk, reflect, wonder, and lay to rest old concerns was not lost on social workers. It seems that whenever our feelings run high, the natural thing to do is to want to talk things over with someone. We go over and over again the feelings of terror we had when we describe being robbed at knife-point. We want to get to the bottom of the worries we have about an ageing mother who is growing increasingly frail and dependent. We bounce around and chatter ecstatically as we want everyone to know about the holiday we've just won in a competition. Strong feelings, whether positive or negative, are hard to contain.

> Freud explored the way in which human behaviour is guided by the unconscious, which inclines one to do things which are not necessarily in one's conscious mind or felt to be in one's best interests ... We are all post Freudians now. We believe that emotions are a critical part of what motivates people. The whole rationalist argument has been knocked on the head. (Orbach 2008: 7)

Psychodynamic approaches believe that unconscious psychological conflicts lie behind many mental health and behavioural problems. The origins of these conflicts, manifested as symptoms, are often found in the experiences of childhood. We are surprisingly bad at knowing the reasons for our actions. Treatment therefore requires that these unconscious memories and conflicts are brought back into consciousness.

Once back in the conscious mind, the patient or client can begin to work on resolving the conflict or the damaging effects of a traumatic experience. Distressing memories can be analyzed and interpreted. The more we can understand the cause of our feelings, particularly those that are disruptive, the more we can make sense of our emotional lives. Things that make sense can be controlled. To be in control of a difficult experience is empowering. It predicts good mental health.

The id

Psychoanalysts believe that much psychopathology results from conflicts between the three major structural parts of the personality: the id, the ego and the superego.

The *id* is that part of the mind concerned with our basic needs and instinctual drives. Food, sex, and survival are the bottom lines of our existence. These very basic and primitive aspects of our make-up give the mind its raw energy. This mental energy is what we call the id. The id therefore is to do with staying alive, seeking pleasure and avoiding pain. All of these biological and bodily drives are psychologically represented at an unconscious level in the id.

These basic drives are so critical to our existence that they act as a powerful unconscious force in all that we do. Left to their own devices, our animal needs, in the form of the id pay no attention to reality or social constraint. The id operates on the *pleasure principle*. Needs and desires, when experienced, feel pressing. They demand immediate satisfaction: 'I want it and I want it now!'. Newborn babies, psychologically speaking, are nothing but id. The id has no sense of right or wrong.

If these urgent, primitive biological forces are not restrained, or at least consciously managed, they can quickly get us into social difficulty. We can't pursue our sexual urges or feelings of aggression willy-nilly. We have to take other people and the social context into account otherwise we become a social menace.

Nevertheless, the id is the ultimate source of all our psychic energy. It is where mind meets body, and psychology connects with biology. Although the id picks up its mental energy and character from our biological drives, and although the id is amoral, selfish and impatient, without it, psychologically speaking, we would be lifeless. It is in the way that we recognize, understand and manage this psychic energy, and the drives and passions that it sponsors that determines our mental health and social competence. This is where the ego comes in.

The ego

The *ego* forms as the id comes up against reality. If the id's demands are to be satisfied, the world of other people and things has to be taken into account. We can't simply be driven by our biological needs, no matter how strongly felt. So, the ego learns to operate on the *reality principle*. We have to become more consciously aware of our needs and the most appropriate ways in which they might be met. The ego therefore learns to act as the executant of the id. To meet the id's needs in ways that are socially appropriate and acceptable, the ego uses thought, calculation and memory.

Some frustration is therefore essential if the ego is to develop. Children learn that more often than not, gratification has to be delayed. The behaviour of children and adults who fail to learn this psychological lesson means that they remain at the mercy of their basic drives and uncontrollable passions. In time many will become the clients of social workers. These are people who are likely to be infantile, impulsive, impatient, aggressive and conflictual. Governed by the id, unrestrained by the ego, they repeatedly end up in behavioural and social difficulty. Infantile demands are not handled well leaving the individual feeling like a frustrated baby – angry, deprived, rageful and helpless.

If the ego is working well, it helps us to cope and to manage relationships. People with weak egos constantly feel under stress as their needs get the better of them. When the ego is unable to manage the environment or control the id, the mind feels overwhelmed – trauma results. Indeed, anything that threatens the ego's integrity is likely to make us feel anxious.

Developing a good understanding of the origins and nature of anxiety features heavily in Florence Hollis's idea of what makes a good social worker:

No single factor in treatment is more important than the worker's keeping his finger on the pulse of the client's anxiety ... What particular things in the client's present or past provoke his anxiousness? How does his anxiety show itself and how does he handle it? In particular: does his anxiety level impel him to unwise acting out? Does it result in increased neurotic or somatic symptomatology? What defences does he use against it? Is he immobilised? Will he run away from treatment? (Hollis 1964: 315)

The superego

The *superego* is the third element of personality structure. As children mature, they are constantly told by parents and other adults what they can and cannot do. They are forever being told what is right and wrong, what is good and bad. The superego is the internalized psychic representation of what is allowed and not allowed. These experiences help us develop a *conscience*. The superego is concerned with social and moral standards.

People who have had authoritarian and punitive parents tend to develop dominant and overbearing superegos. Because they never feel good enough and because they are always being shouted at and being told that they're getting things wrong, these children become riddled with guilt. Guilt is most likely to be felt whenever they sense that one of their basic needs or emotions is in danger of getting the better of them (sex, pleasure, desire, gratification). The superego is therefore in a never ending struggle to keep the id's psychological energy and basic drives battened down and safely padlocked.

Our mental experiences and behaviour are the product of the interaction between the id, ego and superego. When they are in balance, we enjoy good mental health. However, if the ego is weak and feels unable to keep the id's demands in check, anxiety results. If the superego is too dominant, we are conscience-stricken, and guilt ensues.

The defence mechanisms

Anxiety is triggered whenever strong but difficult feelings, normally kept unconscious, threaten to break into and disturb our conscious mind. It is often quite normal to try and defend ourselves psychologically from some of these more distressing anxieties.

The pain associated with the loss of a loved parent might feel unbearable. In an attempt to manage the pain we might try to busy and distract ourselves in work.

In an attempt to ward of the hurt we feel when someone whom we thought was our close friend spends more time with someone else, we might claim not to like her any more. We talk about her dismissively. If we try to convince ourselves that she is no longer important to us, then she might not be able to hurt us. This switch from love to hate, known as *splitting*, is a defensive manoeuvre mounted by the ego. Splitting is what we do when we can't hold two conflicting feelings about someone at the same time, so we give total expression to one and deny the other, only to switch some time later. We talk of people being for us or against, all good or all bad, a fairy godmother or wicked witch, depriving or wonderfully generous.

These attempts by the ego to keep anxiety at bay are known as *defence mechanisms*. Freud first introduced the term. However, it was his youngest daughter, Anna Freud, who published a much more detailed account of the concept in her classic book *The Ego and the Mechanisms of Defence* in 1936.

The concept of defence mechanisms has passed into everyday language. We find ourselves and other people using them all the time as we navigate the emotional turbulence of any typical day. It is only when defence mechanisms begin to distort reality so badly that we begin to worry about an individual's mental health and social competence.

Upwards of 10 or more defence mechanisms are recognized. *Repression*, first discussed by Anna's father, Sigmund, remains the cornerstone of much psychoanalytic work. Whenever we try to keep a difficult and painful thought or feeling out of mind, that thought or feeling is being repressed. It is being kept out of consciousness. If it's a particularly strong feeling, it might show itself in other ways.

For example, early memories of being sexually abused are so painful, so frightening that they can't be thought about. Nevertheless, the powerful feelings don't go away. They remain active in the unconscious and can easily show themselves in other ways. The choice of a male partner might be problematic. The desire to feel safe in the relationship is distorted by the fixated fear and fascination with matters to do with sex. The repeated choice of sexually aggressive men on the face it seems puzzling. It is only when the repressed feelings and traumatic memories are brought to the surface, 'worked through', examined, and *insight* achieved that personal control and conscious choice is recovered. Bringing previously difficult, repressed memories, thoughts and feelings into consciousness leads to recovery.

Displacement is a familiar defence. If I've had a bad day at the office I might come home and behave in an angry, argumentative way with my partner. A strong feeling engendered by one person or setting is displaced on to something or someone else who had nothing to do with the things that caused the original feeling.

Denial occurs when we can't admit how we feel about ourselves, a person or situation. If I've always prided myself on being emotionally strong and independent, the crushing loss and pain experienced when my lover abandons me just isn't the 'me' that I like to present, either to myself or others. I claim to be unaffected, not bothered. I can't bear to be seen as emotionally 'weak'. But feelings that can't be admitted can't be examined, and feelings that go unexamined teach us nothing about life and relationships. Those in constant denial don't grow. They remain emotionally limited. They lack emotional intelligence.

The defence of *projection* occurs when we attack or ridicule someone else for feelings that unconsciously bother us. We project on to them our own fears. The man who is particularly hostile to gay men may harbour uncertainties about his own sexual orientation. He attacks in others that bit of himself that causes him anxiety. Or the adolescent boy whose violent father has left him full of fear, hate and aggression sees other people as threatening and hostile. To defend himself against the perceived but projected threat, he attacks the other, verbally but sometimes even physically.

Reaction formation occurs when an individual holds a very strong critical view on a particular matter such as holding liberal attitudes about sexual behaviour. By excitedly renouncing such attitudes as 'sinful' and 'degenerate', the individual might be revealing his unconsciously strong and anxious feelings about his own sexual urges. To slightly misquote Shakespeare, 'he doth protest too much'.

The psychodynamic therapist's treatment aim is to: 'uncover the unconscious conflicts that cause psychological distress, to bring formerly unconscious material into conscious awareness, and to achieve reintegration of the previously repressed material into the total structure of the personality' (Joseph 2001: 72). Personality structures are changed through resolving these unconscious conflicts.

Interpretation and insight

Interpretation takes place when unconscious thoughts and feelings are made conscious. The client can begin to look at herself more honestly, more realistically and without defence. Successful therapy requires the client to gain *insight* into the origins and causes of his or her psychological problems.

Insight and understanding strengthen the ego in its dealings with the id and superego. In this way, the client recovers control over thoughts and feelings that previously were running out of control. Their burden lightens and they feel better. Given the ambitions of psychoanalytic theory, treatments are rarely short term.

A favoured method is to help the patient talk freely about her thoughts and feelings in a technique known as 'free association'. In the safety of the therapeutic relationship, the patient is encouraged, indeed challenged to explore the repressed conflicts that bubble into consciousness during free association.

The therapist is 'attentive' but neutral in the sense that her own personality doesn't intrude into the relationship. This leaves the client free to 'project' his or her own unconscious thoughts and feelings into the analytic encounter. Alert to these 'projections', the therapist seeks to interpret the unconscious mental forces that are causing the psychological conflict and the problem behaviour. Past and present are thereby linked.

Under the challenge and anxiety of treatment, patients show *resistance*. They might try to change the subject or avoid facing up to the therapist's interpretation. When we feel anxious we might try to keep whatever troubles us out of mind. We resist facing up to it. For example, clients might miss appointments or claim they don't have any thoughts about what's going on in their relationships.

The aim is not a 'cure' by the expert, but to give patients insight into aspects of themselves and what is going on in their mind, understanding the truth about ourselves is potentially liberating and allows us more control of aspects of our lives. Not surprisingly Freud found that his patients were not keen to know or believe unpleasant things about themselves and improvement was often slowed down by resistance. (Bower 2005b: 6)

Transference and counter-transference

As we relate with others, we often have thoughts and feelings about them that are actually based on our relationship experiences with someone else, particularly our parents, other authority figures and significant others. We therefore relate and interact with the person in the current relationship inappropriately. This is the phenomenon of *transference*. Feelings are transferred from one key relationship from the client's past or present on to the therapist or social worker.

For example, if a client felt rejected by her father during childhood, she may unconsciously cast the social worker as rejecting. She interacts with the worker in a surly, defensive, watchful and slightly anxious manner – as if he was the rejecting father. The worker could use this insight to help the client understand the power that unresolved feelings continue to have on present states of mind and current relationships. The 'analysis of the transference' is a key element in treatment.

Counter-transference occurs when therapists or workers find themselves thinking and feeling about a patient in a distinctive and pronounced way. A father who doesn't say much makes the worker feel guilty or a service user with Alzheimer's disease makes a care worker feel irritated. Becoming aware of our feelings about a client can be instructive. They can give us strong clues about what it is about the client that makes us feel the way we do, or why other people react in the ways that they do.

The legacy of Freud and psychoanalysis

Whatever critics feel about Freud in particular and psychoanalytic theory in general, these theories have been immensely influential (for example, in social work, see Bower 2005a). The existence of the unconscious is no longer contested. So much of what the brain is doing by way of processing information and creating mental states takes place outside of conscious awareness.

The idea that we feel anxious whenever our emotions are in conflict is widely accepted. The role that childhood experiences play in shaping our early neurological and psychological development has received much scientific support. This is particularly important when thinking about the damage that childhood abuse and neglect can have on development and mental health.

Psychoanalytic theory's basic ideas continue to evolve. Freud had many followers. Many went on to develop psychoanalytic theories and treatments of their own, not always to Freud's liking. Major figures include Carl Jung, Alfred Adler and Melanie Klein. From around 1930, psychoanalytic theory and practice underwent a huge expansion, especially in the United States. Today, four types of psychoanalytic theory are recognized: Freud's original drive theory; ego psychology; object relations theory; and self psychology.

It is worth saying a little more about object relations theory as it provides a vital link between classic psychoanalytic thinking and attachment theory. The term 'object relations' is not very helpful as it actually refers to the importance of human relationships in our psychological development.

Human infants are born with a strong social and emotional interest in other people ('objects'). Babies are biologically disposed to 'relate' with these 'objects' (significant others). The recognition that the actual quality of the young child's relationships with her primary caregivers is of fundamental importance to her psychological development was a particularly significant insight provided by the Independent School of British psychoanalysts. This School included such major figures as Ronald Fairburn, Michael Balint and Donald Winnicott. Many of their ideas provided the seed-bed for attachment theory and a whole range of modern social supports, treatments and therapies. However, in spite of having their roots in psychodynamic theory, many of these newer developments didn't go down well with traditional psychoanalysts. This hostility was particularly marked in the case of attachment theory and its first author, John Bowlby.

6

Attachment Theory

Attachment behaviour

John Bowlby was a British child psychiatrist. His initial thinking was influenced by the British School of Psychoanalysis. The main departure point, though, was Bowlby's determinedly scientific attempt to understand early parent–child relationships and their impact on development. To this end, and unusually for the time, he studied the ideas being generated by a wide range of developmental sciences including evolutionary theory, ethology, biology, cognitive psychology and systems theory.

Integrating ideas from his clinical work with his increasing knowledge of what other developmental scientists were saying, Bowlby (1969) gradually fashioned what we now know as *attachment theory*. Attachment theory has, and continues to have a major influence on child and family work and more recently adult mental health practice.

Modern developmental attachment theory is also being heavily influenced by the work of neuroscientists. These scientists are interested in how the brain develops and 'hard-wires' itself in the early years, particularly as young children relate with, and are comforted and understood by their primary caregivers (also see Chapter 23 on the brain and its development).

Along with the young of most mammals, human babies are born with a whole range of in-built biological behaviours that increase their chances of survival. One of these is attachment behaviour. Attachment behaviour gets triggered whenever the baby feels frightened, distressed, confused or upset. Loud noises, or feeling hungry, cold, tired, unwell or in danger will trigger attachment behaviour.

The goal of attachment behaviour is to recover closeness to the primary caregiver. This is where safety and comfort lie. As the child matures, separation from, and loss of the primary caregiver itself will also trigger arousal, distress and attachment behaviour. Distance from the source of safety and protection – the mother or father – represents potential danger for any very small and vulnerable mammal, including human babies.

For example, baby lambs that suddenly sense they are some distance from their mother (and therefore in potential danger from predators) experience arousal and distress. This triggers attachment behaviour. The lamb runs as quickly as possible back to the safety of the mother.

Distressed human infants, at least not until they can walk, can't run back to the caregiver at times of need, so they cry and they become behaviourally aroused and distressed. This brings the sensitive caregiver to the baby. Whether lamb or baby, attachment behaviour has achieved its goal of re-uniting infant and caregiver. If the parent is reasonably reliable, sensitive and can be trusted to be there at times of need, the child will develop a secure attachment to the caregiver.

Internal working model

Over time, the infant gradually builds up a sense of her primary caregivers as the source of protection, comfort and emotional regulation. Directing their attachment behaviour to preferred and selected caregivers develops over the first few months of life and properly speaking full-blown attachment behaviour in which the child seeks out selective attachment figures at times of need isn't fully established until the child reaches the age of 7 or 8 months.

As the young child interacts with the significant people in her life, she begins to build up a sense of who she is from the way she is viewed and treated. If she is loved, she will feel lovable and loving. If she is rejected, she will feel unlovable and emotionally alone. If she is valued, she will experience high self-worth. If attachment figures are reliable and responsive, she will learn to trust. Children who are confident that their parents will be there at times of need and have them in mind grow up to be more independent and autonomous.

In these ways, the quality of the relationship becomes internalized by the child and begins to form part of her psychological make-up. The relationship becomes 'mentally represented'. An 'internal working model' of the self, others and relationships develops. The way the self and others are perceived and experienced are products of early relationship experiences with significant others – mothers, fathers, family members. Psychologically speaking, the social outside gets on the mental inside.

The birth of the psychological self

The other key component of attachment theory is to note that at the time the distressed and emotionally dysregulated baby re-engages with the caregiver, the child is in a state of physiological and psychological arousal. Most parents are reasonably sensitive in the care that they give. Winnicott (1960) famously talked of mothering needing only to be 'good enough' for children to thrive.

Attuned, sensitive parents attempt to do something about their child's various needs, upsets and emotional arousals. This involves doing practical things such as feeding the baby, changing a nappy or adding an extra blanket. But importantly it also requires the caregiver to interact with the baby at the sensory, emotional, psychological and interpersonal level. At this key point, the adult mind engages with the young, burgeoning mind of the baby. Psychologists call this mind-to-mind encounter *intersubjectivity*.

The quality of this intersubjective relationship is critical for psychological and emotional development. It is where the child's emotions not only get regulated but also recognized and understood. It is where parent and child play and have fun. It is where parent and child wonder about, and try to make sense of the world of thought, feeling and behaviour, both in the self and in the minds of others. In effect, parents are helping their children become good psychologists and competent social players.

Children who have 'good enough', sensitive and emotionally attuned caregivers develop secure attachments. Knowing that at times of need their parents would wish to be available, they enjoy high levels of confidence, independence and autonomy.

Perhaps even more important, they also develop good social understanding. Children who have experienced secure attachments and psychologically attuned parenting tend to enjoy high self-esteem and develop good social skills and emotional intelligence. These qualities stand them in good stead throughout childhood. These 'resiliences' continue throughout childhood and into adulthood. Children who have shown secure attachment behaviour are less likely to develop behaviour problems. Their development is often described as 'optimal' and their mental health is generally sound.

Insecure attachment patterns and styles

If care which is loving, emotionally attuned, responsive, predictable and consistent leads to secure attachments and optimal psychosocial development, what happens when the caregiving isn't 'good enough'? Attachment researchers recognize a number of insecure attachment patterns. We shall describe two of them: ambivalent and avoidant (Ainsworth et al 1978, Goldberg 1999, Howe et al 1999).

Ambivalent attachments

When parental care is inconsistent and unpredictable, children begin to experience increasing levels of anxiety. These parents are caught up with their own needs and anxieties. As a result their ability to be emotionally attuned and sensitive to the needs of their young child tends to be erratic and poor. Emotional neglect rather than hostility is how the child experiences them. Parents often fail to empathize with their children's moods, needs and feelings. The child is never quite certain where he or she stands. As a result, he or she can become increasingly confused and frustrated. Distress and anxiety lead to a clingy dependence. To this extent, children feel that the world of other people is hard to fathom, difficult to predict and often unreliable. The child therefore feels a degree of frustration, anger and helplessness.

From the child's point of view, love and attention seem to come and go in entirely arbitrary ways. This generates fretful anxiety. In order to increase the likelihood of an otherwise emotionally under-involved parent reacting, children unconsciously develop a range of demanding and attention-seeking, provocative and needful behaviours. They create drama and trouble in an attempt to keep other people involved and interested. Feelings are acted out.

Insensitive and inconsistent care is interpreted by children (and adults who have experienced such care when they were children) to mean that they are ineffective in securing love and sustaining comforting relationships. Children and adults alike conclude that they are not only unworthy of love, but also might be unlovable. This is deeply painful. It undermines self-esteem. It saps self-confidence.

As a result, there is an anxious need for closeness with others but a constant worry that the relationship might not last: 'I need you, but I am not sure I can trust you. You may leave me and cause me pain, so I feel anger as well as fear.' Such thoughts provoke feelings of insecurity, jealousy, conflict and possessiveness in relationships. Intimacy is at the expense of autonomy.

There is a reluctance to let go of others, yet resentment and fear that they may be lost at any time. The result is that people cling to relationships (including those with social workers), yet conduct them with a high level of tension and conflict. Lives, particular for adults who show this pattern, tend to be full of drama, chaos and crisis, many of which will land on the social worker's doorstep.

Avoidant attachments

Children who develop avoidant patterns of attachment have parents who are either indifferent, emotionally rigid or rejecting of their child's needs. Although these parents may respond reasonably well when their child appears content and occupied, they withdraw emotionally or react with irritation when faced with distress and the need for comfort and attention. The clinging, complaining behaviour of children seen in ambivalent attachment relationships serve no purpose in these cooler styles of parenting. Attempts at intimacy only seem to increase parental distance, even rebuff.

Carers of these children encourage independence and de-emphasize dependency. When separated from their parents, avoidant children show few signs of distress. It seems better to become emotionally self-reliant. Negative feelings are contained and rarely expressed. Parental acceptance is achieved by not displaying need and by not being fussy.

Lack of emotional involvement and mutuality mean that both children and avoidant adults find it hard to understand and deal with their own feelings. They may find it difficult to form intimate, emotionally reciprocal relationships. Getting too close to people brings the fear of rejection and pain. So although there is a desire for intimacy, close relationships can cause avoidant people anxiety. In extreme cases this might be dealt with defensively by trying to numb the effects of loneliness and the pain of feeling unlovable by drinking excessively or taking drugs. Avoidant service users are hard to engage. They keep their distance and underplay need. Autonomy appears at the expense of intimacy.

Child abuse, neglect and trauma

Sadly, some children suffer caregiving that neither protects at times of need, nor regulates them at times of distress. Children who suffer parental rejection, abuse, neglect and trauma are at increased risk of poor psychosocial development. Never having enjoyed emotional attunement, they are less likely to be able to understand and regulate their emotions and their arousal (Howe 2005).

If their psychological needs have not been the subject of much interest or curiosity by harsh or disinterested parents, children find it difficult to monitor and make sense not just of their own thoughts and feelings, but also those of other people. This increases the risk of behavioural, relationship and mental health problems across the lifecourse.

Attachment theory and the psychology of intersubjectivity are generating a range of assessment frameworks and intervention practices that are of great relevance for social workers (Howe et al 1999). In particular, attachment theory values the idea that parents should try to connect with their children's emotional needs, mental states and social understanding. Like the good social worker, if parents are to be effective they must learn to be curious as well as caring.

It has to be remembered that children are biologically programmed to relate and be social. It is critical in cases of abuse, neglect and maltreatment that parents are helped to understand this. They need support, guidance and behavioural training in recognizing and enjoying the psychological complexity and amazingness of their child. This can often be difficult for parents who themselves have suffered abuse and neglect, pain and hurt in their own childhoods. This means that social workers also have to help parents develop their own reflective capacities.

First of all, mothers and father are helped to recognize that their young children are busy psychological and emotional beings. Moreover, children love to talk and play with their parents, particularly when it involves being recognized and enjoyed as someone with ideas, thoughts and feelings. Parents who are emotionally attuned and can engage with their children at these various psychological

Behavioural social work

Behaviourists are interested in how behaviours are acquired, how they are maintained, and how they are lost (or extinguished). They are primarily interested in what is currently causing the behaviour, not what might lie in the client's head or psychological past. The interest is in *what* people do, not why they do it. There is a strong belief that behaviour is caused and shaped by the environment, particularly the current environment of other people. Here are a couple of examples given by Macdonald (2007):

> Children for whom cuddles have become a precursor to sexual abuse . . . may well react anxiously to anyone attempting to show affection or reassurance in any way. (p 170)

> Learning can happen unawares, and without anyone intending it. Some children learn that the only way to get their parents' attention is by misbehaving. Others learn that it pays to be aggressive, or that it is best not to be noticed. (pp 170–1).

There is an immediate commonsense appeal about behaviour modification. On an everyday level, it makes sense, it rings true. You are involved in a car crash and feel badly shaken. You may well feel anxious the next time you contemplate getting into a car. In fact, not travelling by car makes you feel relieved, so avoiding cars seems a good idea all round. Or you have a seafood meal in a restaurant and suffer violent stomach ache all night. This is likely to put you off eating seafood which you avoid thereafter. Similarly, we avoid people who in the past have snubbed us.

In each of the above cases, our behaviour has been altered by changes in the way the environment has responded – an unpleasant car crash, poisonous seafood, a hurtful person.

Social learning theory

There are three basic ways in which behaviours are learned. Classical or respondent conditioning was inspired by the early work of Ivan Pavlov and John Watson. Operant conditioning is associated with the ideas of Edward Lee Thorndike and Burrhus Frederic Skinner. Observational learning or modelling was developed by Albert Bandura (1977).

The basic principles of behaviourism are wonderfully simple. The skill is in their creative use and application. Fischer writes that:

In essence, behaviour modification can be defined as the planned, systematic application of experimentally established principles of learning to the modification of maladaptive behavior, specifically to decreasing undesired behaviors and increasing desired behaviors. (Fischer 1978: 157)

Put even more simply, Thorndike (1932: 176) stated that if a behaviour is followed by something pleasurable and satisfying the likelihood of doing that behaviour again is increased. If the behaviour is followed by something nasty or unpleasant, then the likelihood of behaving that way again is decreased. At root, that's all behaviourism is about.

Respondent conditioning

The story begins with Ivan Pavlov's famous experiments on dogs. He taught dogs to salivate at various sounds including the ticking of a metronome and sometimes the ringing of a bell. He first of all noticed that dogs naturally drool when given meat. He then realized that the dogs were actually beginning to salivate as they saw their handlers approach, even before they could even see or smell the food. Pavlov decided to test this association.

At first, when the dogs heard the sound of the metronome or the bell, they made no response. They certainly didn't salivate when they heard ticking metronomes or ringing bells. They only drooled when the food was presented.

So, in the first part of the experiment Pavlov decided that just before the dogs were about to be fed, either a metronome would tick or a bell would ring. And as he hoped, it wasn't long before the dogs began to associate the ringing tone with the arrival of food. In a relatively short time, just the sound of the metronome ticking or the bell ringing, without any food appearing, would cause the dogs to salivate.

Pavlov realized that he had brought about a new response that was not there before. Salivation could now be triggered by sound alone, something that was not previously possible. The dogs had been *conditioned* to drool. They had learned a new behaviour.

Interestingly, there is evidence that social workers who are warm, understanding and responsive are also more likely to be effective and well-regarded by users (Howe 1993). Whatever the final choice of reinforcer, behaviourally speaking, it should be tailor-made for the individual service user.

Two-factor model of behaviour

In practice, behaviourally based interventions tend to combine respondent and operant conditioning techniques. Mowrer (1947) developed what he called the 'two-factor' model. He recognized that in most situations a behaviour might be acquired in the first place through classical conditioning, but it is then maintained through operant conditioning.

For example, a person might now be frightened of dogs after being attacked by a large pit bull terrier in the local park (factor one, classical conditioning). She then began to avoid not only dogs, but also parks, fields and any open space, indeed anywhere she might meet dogs off the leash. This behavioural strategy allowed her to stay relatively calm when she commuted to work or went to the shops. Feeling calm by avoiding dogs and open spaces positively reinforces 'keeping away from dogs and open spaces' behaviour (factor two). When working with patients, behaviour therapists will assess and then treat the problem with both factors in mind.

In summary, the thing to note about behavioural approaches is their insistence on working only with behaviours that can be observed. As you can see, asking the question *why* is not generally of much interest to a behavioural therapist. The preferred questions always begin with *what, how, when* and *where*. These questions can be asked in interview or they might guide the content of a behavioural monitoring diary. What are people actually doing? There is no interest in their unconscious thoughts.

Neither is there is much curiosity about what happened in the distant past. The demand is that the social worker be very concrete and specific when she describes a piece of behaviour. When does it occur? What preceded it? What happened immediately after the behaviour took place (that is, how did the environment respond, in particular how did other people respond)? How often does the behaviour occur? How long does it last for? How intense is the behaviour when it happens?

The basic principles of behaviourism are wonderfully simple. The skill is in their creative use and application. Fischer writes that:

> In essence, behaviour modification can be defined as the planned, systematic application of experimentally established principles of learning to the modification of maladaptive behavior, specifically to decreasing undesired behaviors and increasing desired behaviors. (Fischer 1978: 157)

Put even more simply, Thorndike (1932: 176) stated that if a behaviour is followed by something pleasurable and satisfying the likelihood of doing that behaviour again is increased. If the behaviour is followed by something nasty or unpleasant, then the likelihood of behaving that way again is decreased. At root, that's all behaviourism is about.

Respondent conditioning

The story begins with Ivan Pavlov's famous experiments on dogs. He taught dogs to salivate at various sounds including the ticking of a metronome and sometimes the ringing of a bell. He first of all noticed that dogs naturally drool when given meat. He then realized that the dogs were actually beginning to salivate as they saw their handlers approach, even before they could even see or smell the food. Pavlov decided to test this association.

At first, when the dogs heard the sound of the metronome or the bell, they made no response. They certainly didn't salivate when they heard ticking metronomes or ringing bells. They only drooled when the food was presented.

So, in the first part of the experiment Pavlov decided that just before the dogs were about to be fed, either a metronome would tick or a bell would ring. And as he hoped, it wasn't long before the dogs began to associate the ringing tone with the arrival of food. In a relatively short time, just the sound of the metronome ticking or the bell ringing, without any food appearing, would cause the dogs to salivate.

Pavlov realized that he had brought about a new response that was not there before. Salivation could now be triggered by sound alone, something that was not previously possible. The dogs had been *conditioned* to drool. They had learned a new behaviour.

The technique of getting an animal or an individual to learn a new response or behaviour in this way is often known as *classical conditioning* or *learning theory*. And because the dogs learned to *respond* (salivate) to the new stimulus (the ticking or ringing sound), the technique is also known as *respondent conditioning*.

Developing Pavlov's original research, John Watson believed that many phobias are actually acquired through classical or respondent conditioning.

To illustrate this claim, let's introduce Little Albert. Watson and Raynor (1920) wanted to show how a fear or phobia could develop. Little Albert was 11 months old. He showed no natural fear of furry animals, including scurrying rats or cuddly rabbits. But he was startled and alarmed whenever a loud clanging bar was struck close to him. So what Watson and Raynor decided to do was show Little Albert a tame laboratory rat and at the same time they hit the metal bar producing the loud, startling clang. The experimenters therefore associated a fear reaction with a previously non-frightening stimulus (the tame rat).

It was only a matter of time before Little Albert simply had to see a rat on its own, with no loud clang, for him to become distressed. They had induced in him a fear of rats. Albert had been 'conditioned' to be afraid of rats even though naturally he had shown no such fear. Indeed, there was some evidence that his fear began to 'generalize'. Little Albert began to get upset when he met other furry objects including rabbits. And distressingly that's where we leave Little Albert, never knowing whether he grew up to have a rat phobia, a rabbit phobia or even a fur coat phobia.

These various ways of learning and unlearning behaviours became the basis of a number of behaviour modification techniques. The key question for therapists is: How can a learned or innate behaviour, such as a phobia, be unlearned? It seemed logical to expect that if something pleasant is associated with a response, feeling or behaviour that is currently unpleasant, say a fear of school, then the fear can be extinguished. The undesired behaviour (fear) can be unlearned.

Exposure treatments

Mary Jones was involved in Watson's experiments with Little Albert. She hoped to work with Little Albert and help him unlearn the fears that Watson had induced in the boy. But not surprisingly, Albert's mother wouldn't let any experimental psychologist near her son.

Instead, Jones worked with another little boy, Peter, who was frightened of a variety of white objects, including rabbits. She tried the technique in which a pleasant stimulus (for example, a sweet) was introduced at the same time as the child was exposed to the feared object. By working in gradual stages, Jones (1925) was able to help Peter lose his fear of white objects including rabbits.

These pioneering experiments by Jones represented the beginnings of behaviour therapy. However, it was Joseph Wolpe (1990) who developed and refined her early insights. The result was a therapeutic procedure that he called graduated deconditioning, later known as *systematic desensitization*. Today, we refer to this broad range of interventions as exposure treatments. Graded exposure treatments refer to interventions that expose the client to the feared situation in a gradual manner, either in imagination or for real.

The treatment has three stages:

- relaxation training including deep breathing;
- construction of a fear hierarchy; and
- a new learning process.

Anxiety and fear are incompatible with pleasure and feeling relaxed. Taking advantage of this finding, the idea is to introduce a positive, pleasurable experience that outweighs the negative, unpleasant experience. The client is first taught to *relax* using a variety of techniques that best suit him or her. These often involve learning to relax both muscles and mind.

The next stage requires the client to construct a hierarchy of fear in which the most feared situation is scored at say a 100%. Things that cause no anxiety whatsoever are rated at 0%. In between are all those other situations that cause varying degrees of fear, each with their own distress rating.

A person with a social phobia may be able to look out of the window and see people passing without anxiety (fear rating = 0%). However, she experiences some distress when walking down the street. Waiting at a bus stop where there might be other people queuing would cause considerable anxiety (say 40% fear rating). Being in a busy shop would be even worse (fear rating = 70%). However, the highest ratings are given for social situations where the individual might have to interact and talk with people – a job interview, a party, a date (fear rating 100%).

The client is first asked to imagine the lowest anxiety state, say walking down the street (an experience rated at 5% anxiety) while practising the relaxation technique. This is repeated until the thought, or actual experience of being in the street causes no anxiety. So what was a 5% anxiety level is now the new zero level. The next stage up in the original fear hierarchy is now 'visited' using the same technique. This incremental approach is pursued until finally the previously most feared situations – the shopping mall, the interview, the party, the date – are anticipated without anxiety.

Some therapists will actually ask the patient to progress through each stage for real, not as an imagined exercise but *in vivo*. In the case of the social phobic client, as well as practising relaxation techniques, a friend or reassuring therapist might initially accompany the individual as they negotiate each level of the fear hierarchy. The increasing feeling of confidence and control in situations that used to cause anxiety acts as a further pleasurable stimulus.

Operant conditioning

Classical or respondent conditioning shows us how a stimulus can produce a *new behaviour* or eliminate an undesired behaviour. However, there is another way of shaping a person's behaviour. This technique can increase the frequency, duration or intensity of an existing behaviour. The technique is known as *operant conditioning* or *instrumental conditioning*.

It was Thorndike who found that if a behaviour leads to a positive or desired outcome, it is likely to be repeated in similar situations in the future. For example, if someone continues to behave in a certain way, there must be something or someone that helps keep that behaviour going. If every time a toddler cries he's told to shut up and given a packet of crisps, it will not be long before the child learns that yelling produces a reaction and a bag of crisps. In contrast, if a behaviour produces a negative or unpleasant outcome, it is less likely that it will be repeated in similar situations.

It was Skinner who developed Thorndike's ideas even further. He called any environmental response that increased a behaviour a *reinforcer*. He called any environmental response that decreased the occurrence of a behaviour a *punishment*.

Thus, whereas in classical conditioning the environment (say, the appearance of a spider or snake) causes a behavioural reaction (fear), matters are reversed in operant conditioning.

For example, dogs can be trained to come to heel at the sound of a whistle using biscuits as a reinforcer. The desired behaviour (the dog coming to heel at the sound of a whistle) 'causes' the environment to respond (a rewarding dog biscuit appears). The behaviour has 'operated' on (that is, triggered a response from) the environment. The biscuit acts as a *positive reinforcement*. It has rewarded 'responding to the whistle' behaviour. The dog's behaviour has led to a *consequence* – the appearance of a biscuit. In short, the behaviour has had a pay-off which, because it produces pleasure, makes it worth repeating. Thus, under these rewarding conditions 'responding to the whistle and coming to heel' behaviour is very likely to increase.

Skinner, summarizing matters, simply stated: 'Behavior is shaped and maintained by its consequences' (1971: 23). For example: A lonely 82 year old woman was rarely visited by her son. One day she accidently put a supermarket chilled meal in her shopping bag without paying for it. This lead to minor, quite sympathetic police and medical involvement and a visit from her son. This marked the beginning a spate of deliberate shoplifting, each time followed by a visit from her erstwhile neglectful son and daughter-in-law.

Many of the problem behaviours shown by children are the result of parents unwittingly but *positively reinforcing* unwanted behaviours. Temper tantrums, food refusal, crying when left alone in bed are examples of behaviours that might have been shaped by parental responses. For example, when a child acts in silly way and starts jumping up and down on the furniture, the parent intervenes, even if the intervention is a verbal telling off. However, when the child is playing happily showing no distress or upset, the parent ignores him, goes into the kitchen or sneaks off to the local shop.

From the child's point of view, any parental recognition, acknowledgement or interest is better than none. Parental attention nearly always acts as a reinforcer. If the parent responds or supplies recognition, acknowledgement or interest only when the child misbehaves, in effect they are reinforcing naughty and unwanted behaviour.

On the other hand, if the parent ignores the child when he or she has painted a picture of which they are proud, or managed to complete a difficult puzzle, in effect the parent is giving no reward for self-directed play. The child learns that naughty behaviour gets you noticed and good behaviour means that you are ignored. By responding in the ways that they do, parents 'shape' their children's behaviour.

Sounding perhaps a little odd at first, it is also possible to *increase* behaviours by *removing an aversive stimuli* or unpleasant response. This is known as a *negative reinforcement* (which is not to be confused with punishment). For example, if speed cameras are removed from motorways, there is a likely to be an increase in fast driving.

In contrast, 'punishments' in the behavioural sense are environmental responses to a behaviour that lead to a *decrease* of that behaviour. *Positive punishments* involve the *introduction of an aversive response*. A child is 'fined' his pocket money if he is aggressively rude to his parents. Here, the hope is that the surly behaviour will stop. *Negative punishment* describes the *removal of a response that decreases a behaviour*. For example, if a teacher stops praising a child who persists with a difficult task, the child might give up trying.

Simply *ignoring a behaviour* can also lead to its decline or *extinction*. In a variation of his classic experiments, Pavlov rang the bell again and again but this time without the appearance of food. Gradually the dogs stopped salivating when they heard the bell ring. The dogs had 'unlearned' their original conditioned salivating behaviour.

Similarly, in cases in which a parent is complaining of a child's difficult, unruly behaviour, a relatively simple behaviour modification programme might involve advising the parent to ignore the child's display of bad behaviour (an *extinction procedure*) and *reinforce* examples of good, desired behaviour with positive attention, praise, encouragement, and admiration (*positive reinforcement procedures*). Punishment procedures are rarely advised and can often be counter-productive.

In short, what operant conditioning describes is the modification of behaviour so that there is either more or less of it, depending on what consequences follow that behaviour.

The ABC of behaviour modification

Behavioural techniques first require a careful assessment of the problem: specify exactly what happens. Who behaves in what manner before, during and after the emission of the undesired behaviour?

This is the ABC of behaviour: antecedents → behaviour → consequences. Observations are made and questions asked about the frequency, duration, and intensity of the behaviour. Assessments therefore need to be clear about *who* does *what, where, when, how often,* and *with whom* (Sheldon 1998: 30).

By re-shaping the way the (social) environment reacts to behaviours, the aim is to decrease conduct that is problematic and increase behaviours that are desired. In such ways are behaviours shaped and modified. The basics are therefore as easy as A–B–C:

Antecedents: What happens before the behaviour, what expectations might be present?
Behaviour: Describe the behaviour itself in very specific, concrete detail.
Consequences: What happens immediately after the behaviour? How do other people respond? What's reinforcing it or suppressing it?

The problem behaviour can then be modified by changing either what happens immediately *before* the behaviour occurs – that is change the *antecedents* (classical or respondent conditioning). Or the problem behaviour can be modified by changing what happens immediately *after* the behaviour occurs – that is change the *consequences* (operant conditioning).

The aims of intervention also need to be couched in very clear, specific behavioural terms. Saying that a father has to improve his parenting skills is too vague. Much better to say what he has to do more of, less of, when, with whom, and how often.

Being clear about current behaviours and future desired behaviours means that the worker can measure and evaluate the success of the intervention. After the intervention, is there less of the undesired behaviour and more of the desired behaviour? Behavioural social workers are very good at being clear and specific about their hypotheses, aims, interventions, evaluations and outcomes.

Part of the art of behaviour modification is finding the right reinforcer or reward. Reinforcers can be food, money, privileges, treats or tokens (gold stars, points).

However, the most potent reinforcers are social. Praise, attention and recognition are great rewards for children and adults alike. Truax actually (1966) felt that counsellors and therapists who offer high levels of empathy, warmth and genuineness are more effective because these qualities act as positive reinforcers.

Interestingly, there is evidence that social workers who are warm, understanding and responsive are also more likely to be effective and well-regarded by users (Howe 1993). Whatever the final choice of reinforcer, behaviourally speaking, it should be tailor-made for the individual service user.

Two-factor model of behaviour

In practice, behaviourally based interventions tend to combine respondent and operant conditioning techniques. Mowrer (1947) developed what he called the 'two-factor' model. He recognized that in most situations a behaviour might be acquired in the first place through classical conditioning, but it is then maintained through operant conditioning.

For example, a person might now be frightened of dogs after being attacked by a large pit bull terrier in the local park (factor one, classical conditioning). She then began to avoid not only dogs, but also parks, fields and any open space, indeed anywhere she might meet dogs off the leash. This behavioural strategy allowed her to stay relatively calm when she commuted to work or went to the shops. Feeling calm by avoiding dogs and open spaces positively reinforces 'keeping away from dogs and open spaces' behaviour (factor two). When working with patients, behaviour therapists will assess and then treat the problem with both factors in mind.

In summary, the thing to note about behavioural approaches is their insistence on working only with behaviours that can be observed. As you can see, asking the question *why* is not generally of much interest to a behavioural therapist. The preferred questions always begin with *what, how, when* and *where*. These questions can be asked in interview or they might guide the content of a behavioural monitoring diary. What are people actually doing? There is no interest in their unconscious thoughts.

Neither is there is much curiosity about what happened in the distant past. The demand is that the social worker be very concrete and specific when she describes a piece of behaviour. When does it occur? What preceded it? What happened immediately after the behaviour took place (that is, how did the environment respond, in particular how did other people respond)? How often does the behaviour occur? How long does it last for? How intense is the behaviour when it happens?

reasonably in relationships, then at some level I'm going to be OK, I'm going to get on, I'm going to be liked. I have some confidence in my own inherent worth.

But what if my past experiences have undermined my self-esteem and confidence? What happens to my cognitive schemas? How do I perceive and experience myself in relation to others. Aaron Beck and his colleagues (Beck et al 1990) cite the example of Sue:

Sue's boyfriend, Tom, was working on some chores in another room. He was making a lot of noise, including banging. Sue interpreted this as 'Tom is making a lot of noise because he's angry at me.' She had a 'negative attributional bias'. She processed the information through a schema that said 'When people are noisy, it means that they are angry, and in this case angry with me.' She had other schemas that supported this interpretation. 'If people reject me, I will be all alone.' 'Being alone will be devastating.' And deep down, beneath all of this, she had a schema that made her believe that she was unlovable. So when she hears Tom making noises, she immediately feels anxious. 'Being noisy means he's angry with me about something. That frightens me. He's rejecting me. I'm unlovable. I'll be left all alone and I couldn't cope with that.'

There is a lot of distorted and negative thinking going on here. A cognitive therapist would want to help Sue examine the rationality of these thoughts. Given what he knows about the objective reality of the situation, Beck suspects that Tom's loud hammering is better explained by realizing that he's simply feeling exuberant.

Rational emotive therapy

It was Albert Ellis (1962) who first proposed that problem behaviours and emotional distress are the result of irrational beliefs held about the self, others and situations. He developed what is now known as *rational emotive therapy*. Change how you think and you'll feel better. This is captured nicely in the title of one of his self-help tapes: *21 Ways to Stop Worrying and Start Living* (1972). The task of the therapist, therefore, is to help the individual change his beliefs from ones that are negative and irrational to ones that are positive and realistic.

Ellis says that human beings have three fundamental goals: to survive; to be relatively free from pain; and to be reasonably satisfied and content. It is therefore rational to argue that any thought, feeling or behaviour that interferes with these goals is irrational.

If someone is feeling anxious, depressed, or self-destructive, the thoughts or feelings that sustain these cognitive-emotional states are irrational. They have to be challenged. The therapist must dispute them. Clients have to be confronted with how they are actually contributing to their own distress.

Nelson-Jones (1995: 263) gives some wry examples from Ellis's own life. Naturally shy with women, the 19 year old Ellis challenged himself to visit the Bronx Botanical Gardens and sit on a bench and initiate a conversation with whoever was sitting next to him, particularly if the person was a young woman of his own age. He repeated this task a hundred times until he no longer felt anxious and reserved at the prospect of talking to women.

> Ellis recalls how he and his sister coped with their father's absences and their mother's neglect. His sister failed to develop the same problem-solving skills that he did partly because 'she was born with a whiny, demanding, injustice-collecting temperament and . . . consequently she *chose* to make the worst of her childhood conditions'. Thus, his sister was partly responsible for her misery by consciously or unconsciously choosing to victimise herself to 'what is going on . . . in the world'. (Nelson-Jones 1995: 267, emphasis original)

Asking clients to carry out tasks that test out or contradict their beliefs, such as those prescribed by Ellis for himself, is now part of most treatment procedures. However, for the cognitive therapist, the idea is not to carry out tasks to alter behaviour *per se* but *to change thinking*.

Changes in behaviour help modify beliefs – that nothing terrible happens when you give a public speech, that no danger is met when you go out and shop and meet people that nothing really awful happens when you start an innocent conversation with a young woman. The aim is therefore not to help the client think positively but realistically (Trower et al 1988: 7).

Clearly not one to suffer fools gladly, particularly fools who irrationally make their own lives miserable, Ellis felt fully justified in developing his *disputatious* method of challenging his client's self-defeating thoughts, feelings and beliefs about the inevitability of their own unhappy condition.

He suggests that therapists be on constant look out for the words *must, ought, should, have to* and *got to* whenever used by clients. 'I must behave like this or my partner will reject me.' 'I have to repeat my compulsive behaviours or something terrible will happen.' These self-imposed behavioural imperatives – *must, have to, got to* – tell the counsellor that the client is not admitting that their belief, thought or feeling may be irrational. There may be no justifiable logic to them.

Even more perverse, once locked into these loops of negativity, people make themselves even more anxious about being anxious, more depressed about being depressed, more guilty about feeling guilty (Nelson-Jones 1995: 270). So by confronting clients and then teaching them to recognize their own irrational beliefs, clients are then taught to confront and challenge their own illogical thoughts, feelings and beliefs.

Challenge negative thinking

Beck and colleagues (1979) also felt that negative ways of thinking that affect mood are illogical. If we are in a gloomy mood, we tend to magnify our difficulties. We tend to see everything in a negative light. 'Everything I do goes wrong.' 'No-one likes me.' 'My life is a failure. It's not worth living.' These global, negative beliefs about the self have to be disputed. Where is the evidence for their truth?

If we are in a negative mind-set, we ignore or deny the positives in our life. In such moods, we actually seem incapable of being optimistic. We become passive and fatalistic. There is no point in trying because anything we do will be a waste of time. Our thoughts are distorted and the cognitive distortions begin to colour how we see, think and feel.

The task of the therapist is to challenge the basis for these negative thoughts. Realistically, where is the evidence for all this negativity?

The treatment process

Like most scientifically based approaches, cognitive therapy is very structured. It tends to be brief, typically involving a maximum of 20 sessions usually spread over several months.

Beck and Weishaar (1989, cited in Joseph 2001: 106–8), note five steps in cognitive therapy:

1. Learning to monitor negative, automatic thoughts.
2. Learning to recognize the connection between cognition, affect and behaviour (that is how thought affects feeling and feeling affects behaviour).
3. Examining the evidence for and against distorted automatic thoughts.
4. Substituting more reality-oriented interpretations for these biased cognitions.
5. Learning to identify and alter the beliefs that predispose a person to distort their experiences.

First, it is important to develop a warm, collaborative relationship with the service user. The social worker is very open and up-front with the user. The theory and the basis on which the treatment works is explained and honestly set out. In fact, it's important for the client to understand how behavioural and cognitive treatments work.

Once explained, most people realize that there is a lot of common sense in the approach. We all recognize that when a behaviour is praised and encouraged, we're much more likely to repeat that behaviour. We also know that we can be our own worst enemy when we start to think negatively.

Service users are asked to become aware of, name and then fully describe their negative thoughts or feelings. This helps them connect with their inner emotional selves. The social worker explores, examines and tests what the user is saying and whether or not there is any rational basis for saying what is being said.

Beck's cognitive therapies have been particularly successful in the treatment of depression and many of the anxiety disorders (Beck and Emery 1985). Depressed people tend to think negatively about everything and everyone. When they reflect and remember, it is always negative thoughts and memories that are brought to mind. They view themselves as worthless and unlovable. The future always looks bleak. It is the job of the therapist to alter these negative thinking patterns.

Automatic negative thoughts

It is all too easy for clients who suffer depression or anxiety to slip into Automatic Negative Thoughts (ANTs). The first thing that the social worker must do is teach the client user to monitor and recognize each and every time they find themselves slipping into depressed and negative thinking.

The worker will ask the user to test the validity of the negative thought. Is there any objective evidence to justify such an all-consuming gloomy or worried outlook? The client may say that everything they've ever done has been a waste of time. They doubt that anyone cares whether they exist or not. Such extreme negative thoughts tend to be exaggerated. They rarely stand up to close scrutiny. It is these negative thoughts that are constantly brought to mind making the client feel either anxious or depressed, a failure or a hopeless parent, unlovable or incompetent.

There is therefore a tendency to think in extreme and distorted terms. All-or-nothing thinking is common: 'If I can't get back together with my partner I might as well be dead.'

Overgeneralizations frequently occur: 'Everything I do is a failure. There's no point in trying.' Any positive thinking is dismissed: 'I know my son behaved quite well yesterday, but that was a fluke. It won't happen again.'

Socratic questions

Clients are then invited to consider if there might not be another, less negative way of thinking about themselves or their situation. Techniques are introduced that help the client avoid always thinking negatively.

To help clients change their thought patterns, a certain style of questioning is employed sometimes referred to as Socratic dialogue after the manner of questioning employed by the ancient Greek philosopher, Socrates. Whereas Ellis would actively dispute the rationality of holding an irrational belief, Beck would simply question the client. He would encourage description, expansion and evaluation of the belief.

The dialogue leads the client through a series of questions that help him or her to become aware of distorted and negative thoughts.

These negative thoughts are then gently challenged. 'Where's the evidence for this belief?' 'What's the evidence for thinking that you're a total failure?' 'What do you have to lose if you do the thing that you're afraid to do?' 'What do you have to gain if you do the thing you're afraid to do?' 'What's the worst thing that could happen if you do mess up?' 'What's another way of looking at the situation?'

Here is an example of work with a depressed patient used by Beck et al (1979: 265–6) to illustrate the method. The patient is guided by the questions to recognize that the initial statement is inaccurate. The irrational or negative thought is queried:

Patient:	I think anyone who isn't concerned with what others think would be socially retarded and functioning at a pretty low level.
Therapist:	Who are the two people you admire most? (The therapist knew the answer from previous discussion)
Patient:	My best friend and boss.
Therapist:	Are these two over concerned with others' opinions?
Patients:	No. I don't think that either one cares at all what others think.
Therapist:	Are they socially retarded and ineffective?
Patient:	I see your point. Both have good social skills and function at high levels.

By querying each negative thought, the therapist is seeking to undermine the tendency to keep thinking in a depressed or hopeless fashion.

The ABC of cognitive therapy

Many of us have a tendency to see our emotions, particularly unhealthy negative emotions as a direct consequence of some prior event. Someone jumps the queue; we get angry. The interview with a service user doesn't go well; we feel depressed. A cognitive approach argues that lying between an event and an unhealthy negative emotion are thoughts and beliefs. It is the way we think about the event that actually leads to the negative emotion. This gives us another A–B–C theory, this time of emotion: Antecedent–Belief–Consequence.

At its simplest level, this theory suggests that if one's beliefs about A or C are positive, one feels 'cheery' and does cheery things; if one's beliefs about A or C are negative, one feels 'yukkie' and does things characterised as 'yukkie'. (Kushlick et al 1998: 167)

So the idea is to change the person's belief about either the 'antecedent' or 'consequence' by softly, but persistently challenging and disputing them. If the individual can be helped to see that their belief is a product of their own thinking and not some objective, immutable, forever state of affairs, then they can change the emotional consequence.

A client may feel they are 'worthless' and this is depressing. It is this belief that has to be questioned. Do you really feel totally worthless every minute of every day? It isn't difficult to identify moments when the individual doesn't feel totally worthless. What about when you picked up an old woman's walking stick that had fallen over? What did you feel like then? What was the momentary belief that you had that made you feel helpful (and therefore of value)?

It is these positive beliefs that have to be identified, worked on, and expanded. People who get trapped in loops of negative and unhealthy emotions (anxiety, depression, anger, panic) apply them globally to everything they do and everything that happens. This global, over-generalization has to be challenged.

Once a detailed description and analysis of the behaviour, thought or feeling is achieved, together the social worker and client work out how to bring about change and move forward. The client is asked to review each session. They are invited to draw conclusions. They are asked if they have been able to make better sense of some of their thoughts, feeling and behaviour. New, more positive ways of thinking about the self, the situation and the solution are discussed, rehearsed and tried.

Behavioural and cognitive practitioners have much to offer social work. They have a long history and a handsome track record of evidence informed research. It is no surprise, then, to learn that cognitive and behavioural approaches long ago combined forces to offer cognitive-behavioural therapy.

9
Cognitive-behavioural Social Work

Thoughts, feelings and behaviour

It soon became apparent that combining the insights of both behavioural and cognitive psychology generated a particularly powerful set of ideas. Today, behavioural and cognitive therapies are linked in a package known as cognitive behavioural therapy or CBT. It is one of the mainstream treatments used by mental health specialists. The evidence base for the effectiveness of CBT is now very solid.

According to Trower and colleagues (1988: 4), there are three main assumptions underlying cognitive behavioural approaches: '(a) that emotions and behaviour are determined by thinking; (b) that emotional disorders result from negative and unrealistic thinking; and (c) that by altering this negative and unrealistic thinking emotional disturbance can be reduced.'

Behavioural and cognitive therapies have been particularly effective in treating problems of mood such as anger, depression, anxiety disorders including phobias, and conduct disorders. CBT has been employed to help people control their anger and offending behaviour. The treatment focus is on encouraging offenders to think before they act. CBT based approaches have attracted the interest of many clinical psychologists, psychiatrists, social workers, social care workers, probation officers, youth justice workers and counsellors.

In general, treatment combines the best of both behavioural and cognitive therapies. Irrational beliefs and automatic negative thinking are challenged. Reinforcement procedures are used to encourage more positive behaviours.

Cognitive-behavioural social work

Parker (1998) gives a helpful example of using cognitive and behavioural techniques in a case of elder abuse.

Mr and Mrs Walker have been married for over 50 years. Mr Walker now suffers arthritis and Padget's disease. Two years ago Mrs Walker – Jean – banged her head. Although she made a physical recovery, her behaviour has become more and more difficult to manage for her husband. She is tearful, depressed, sometimes confused, follows Mr Walker everywhere, and continually packs and unpacks clothes in a suitcase.

Mr Walker feels under increasing stress. His wife's behaviour can make him angry, sometimes to the point of feeling aggressive. He shouts at her crossly. He then feels guilty and distressed.

The aim of the social worker, health visitor and doctor was cognitively to reduce Mr Walker's feelings of stress and anger. They also planned a number of behavioural changes. These included finding ways of distracting and adapting some of Mrs Walker's more trying behaviours.

As part of the assessment, a functional analysis of Mr Walker's anger was undertaken using a behavioural ABC recording sheet. In this case the B is for Behaviour (Antecedent-Behaviour-Consequence). Anger was operationalized as shouting and swearing at Mrs Walker. Table 9.1 shows an example from Mr Walker's recording sheet (Parker's 1998: 251).

A pattern became clear. Mr Walker became angry, shouted and swore, felt guilty, and then gave Mrs Walker apologetic and remorseful attention. The suitcase packing and unpacking behaviour occurred when Mrs Walker was at a loose end. The suitcase behaviour actually led to Mr Walker spending more time with his wife, thus positively reinforcing the activity.

Table 9.1 An example of a recording sheet

A Antecedent	B Behaviour	C Consequence
Jean kept mumbling something about her mother. I was trying to get the washing-up done after lunch, but she wouldn't leave me alone.	I told her she was a stupid old cow and that she'd better go away and let me get on before I put her in a home.	She burst into tears. I had to calm her down, and so sat and cuddled her. I said sorry.

When [Mr Walker] became angry and frustrated, he felt he was letting down his wife, his family and his values. He *believed* he was bad, weak, and felt ashamed that he responded in this way. Mr Walker's *beliefs* about his anger led to him trying harder, and increased his physical stress and self-blame and loathing, and this increased his mental stress ... Mr Walker believed that he was a bad husband who was not fulfilling what was expected of him by himself, his family or society. This in turn led to affective distress and maladaptive behavioural responses. His shouting, swearing, and belittling of his wife reinforced his *belief* in his inadequacies, which led to greater frustration and greater possibility for his maladaptive response. By altering the contingencies and *adapting his thinking* processes, change was possible. (Parker 1998: 252 and 255, emphases added)

Cognitive-behavioural help included anger management in which Mr Walker learned to recognize the build up of his anger. He then 'self-talked' himself into less negative beliefs. He also learned techniques to relax whenever he felt under stress.

If Mrs Walker appeared restless, she was given more acceptable tasks to carry out, such as tidy up a drawer or pack old newspapers away. This reduced the annoying suitcase behaviour. If she did begin the packing/unpacking behaviour, Mr Walker was to count to 10 and then ignore it. Mr Walker also agreed to sit down with his wife for one hour each afternoon to look through photograph albums and other memorabilia.

Tried and tested

The strong evidence-based underpinnings of behavioural and cognitive interventions has made them particularly attractive to social workers who are more science-oriented. There is a demand that problems are defined and measured very precisely. Describe the behaviour in concrete detail. Note when, with whom and how often it occurs. Observe what occurs before, during and after the behaviour's appearance. The cognitive-behavioural social worker is willing to be more directive than the average practitioner. She is happy to make concrete suggestions (Macdonald 2007: 175). Do this, try that, and let's see what happens.

All of this makes cognitive-behavioural social work, with its impressive evidence-base supporting the effectiveness of much of what it does, a top-rank social work theory. Odd then, that it is not as widely and thoroughly taught as it ought to be.

> The results of systematic reviews and experiments show that in juvenile justice and probation, in cases of depression, in relapse prevention, in schizophrenia, in the field of child behavioural problems, in helping families cope with an autistic child, and so forth, cognitive-behavioural approaches never come second to anything. It should therefore be the preferred therapeutic option. Perversely, and unethically, it is probably the approach least likely to be taught on qualifying courses, even though relevant text-books aimed specifically at social workers have been in print since the mid-1960s. (Sheldon and Macdonald 2009: 64)

Cognitive behaviourists, with some justification, get very cross with any theory or approach that isn't supported by tested and testable research-based evidence. 'Infuriatingly,' fumes Cigno (1998: 265), '... alongside careful studies which should increasingly make it difficult to do our own thing or follow fashion rather than heed research findings ... a certain amount of nonsense is being taught and practised'. Quite what nonsense Cigno had in mind isn't clear, but no doubt we shall be looking at more of it, possibly favourably, later on in this book.

We have noted that the 1970s was a time when social casework based on psychoanalytic thinking was beginning to come under fierce attack from a number of directions. Psychoanalytically-based casework tended to be a long term and therefore expensive treatment. There was pressure, particularly in the US where much social work was funded by health insurance, to develop shorter and cheaper psychotherapies.

So, psychoanalytic-based casework began to fall out of favour, initially on grounds of cost, then effectiveness, before finally being subject to an ideological assault by Marxist social workers.

However, one of the most interesting and influential theories to emerge at this time was neither sponsored by a rival psychological premise (behavioural social work) nor inspired by an ideological stance (radical social work). Cheekily, it was conceived in the bosom of psychoanalytic casework itself.

It was while William Reid and Ann Shyne (1969) were carrying out research into the effects of brief and extended casework that the beginnings of a task based approach began to take shape. To their initial surprise not only did brief interventions seem to work well, but also some of the traditional long term treatments seemed to make matters worse the longer they continued. So what was going on?

10

Task-centred Work

The pragmatic approach

Throughout the 1960s American social workers were experimenting with help that was more problem-focussed, advice-based and short-term. Philosophically, America has always had a taste for sharp, business-like approaches to problem-solving.

In the first half of the twentieth century, John Dewey, an American philosopher of education, was fashioning a problem-solving approach. Whereas Freud and psychoanalysis concentrated on people's emotional make-up, Dewey and others focussed on their cognitive capacities: thought rather than feeling, *changing what people do* rather than how they feel.

Dewey believed that people solve problems first by reflecting on them. Then they systematically analyze the problem situation in which they find themselves. We are naturally motivated and energized to try and change situations that are not to our liking. Whenever we find ourselves facing a difficulty the first thing we do is ponder and think about it. Only after some reflection and analysis do we begin to plan how best to tackle it. The pragmatic, problem-solving approach therefore has several stages.

If we are to resolve a problem, the first thing we do is recognize, define and specify it in more detail. We have to fathom its make-up and character.

Having weighed up the problem, we then think of possible solutions. Some solutions will be ruled out as impractical or unlikely to work. However, those that hold out promise will be tried. If we succeed in solving the problem, those solutions to those problems will be remembered and used again.

Dewey argued that this is the way most of us try to deal with problems – recognize them, examine them, define and describe them, consider possible solutions, choose a solution, and carry it out.

Car mechanics faced with an engine failure, doctors assessing a patient's illness, builders wondering how best to support a heavy roof – they all use a form of Dewey's reflective, problem-solving approach. Even in the midst of the 'psychiatric deluge' many social workers were struck by the eminent sense and practicality of using such *pragmatic* approaches to solving problems. The approach is direct. It tends to be short and purposeful. It doesn't worry about the client's deeper psychological condition.

The problem-solving approach

The most famous exponent of what became known as the 'problem-solving approach' in social work was Helen Harris Perlman (1957). Writing in the 1950s, she was still deriving inspiration from some of the more recent developments in psychodynamic thinking. Ego-psychology in particular was throwing up interesting ideas.

As we have seen, the ego operates on the 'reality principle'. The ego is that bit of the psyche that has to deal with and function in the external environment – the real world. It is at this point that the pragmatic approach of Dewey and the post-Freudian ideas of an autonomous, conflict-resolving ego meet.

Perlman found the ground where the two theories bumped into each other to be particularly fertile. She wanted to marry education with therapy, Dewey with Freud. She saw life as a 'problem-solving process'. She wanted to boost the ego's capacities so that it could problem solve more efficiently and more effectively. She wanted people to be able to cope.

The interest here is that Perlman anticipated many of the problem-solving and solution-focused approaches that now populate so many corners of social work practice. She certainly paved the way for task-centred social work. She was absolutely clear that the person with the problem is best placed to solve it. 'That person,' she says, 'with his subjective reading of and reaction to his problem(s) must also be his own problem-solver. The problem cannot be dealt with except through him, with him, and by involvement of his powers' (Perlman 1970: 131).

When we first get into difficulty, most of us typically experience problems as big and overwhelming. We don't know where to start. It all seems too much. We collapse into helpless inertia or distressed panic. Perlman was clear that in most cases we can only proceed by breaking a problem down into smaller, manageable bits. Although we need to keep the overall problem in mind, we achieve success by dealing with the component 'bits' of the problem one at a time, step by step, in a planned sequence.

When we are in a crisis, we want to get out of the troubling situation as fast as possible. However, a feeling of being in crisis can also paralyze us. Nevertheless, because the situation at such times is so unpleasant, we are highly motivated to change it.

Brief casework

It was this old insight that came to mind when Reid and Shyne (1969) were analyzing data derived from their study of 120 families who had sought help for a variety of family relationship problems. The families had been randomly assigned to one of two types of treatment. One was a relatively traditional, psycho-analytically oriented and open-ended treatment programme. The other was an abbreviated, short-term casework intervention of eight sessions. The results came as something of a surprise.

On several key measures, the clients receiving the brief burst of casework achieved more positive change than those being worked with on an open-ended, longer lasting intervention. Among the reasons that Reid and Shyne gave for this unexpected result was that when faced with a problem we tend to make most changes in the first few days and weeks. And of course, if there is also a time-limit to do something about it, nothing concentrates the mind like a dead-line.

These findings and their interpretation build on the problem-solving tradition. However, the tradition up to this point was still borrowing heavily from psychiatry, clinical psychology and counselling. But what Reid and his colleagues then did was a rare thing. They generated a social work theory and practice that was home grown. Initially called task-centred casework it evolved in what today we call task-centred work or brief therapy.

Task-centred work

Reid and Epstein's book, *Task-centred Casework* first published in 1972 was a landmark text. It made a significant impact. For the field social worker struggling to understand the fascinating but often difficult world of psychodynamic theory, the directness of task-centred work was a delight. Here was a 'how-to-do-it' theory that seemed straightforward and simple. Certainly the basic ingredients were easy to understand. So what was this theory, this approach to social work that went down so well with practitioners?

We had learned from Reid and Shyne's research that when in crisis people are motivated to change. Deadlines help. And people generally have ideas of their own about what might sort things out, but they lack the confidence or structure to follow them through. The problem-solving nature of task-centred work helps users to recognize that they have the ability to do something about their situation. It is an empowering approach.

Out of these initial findings emerged the key elements of task-centred work: targets, tasks and time limits. Service users have problems – these are the *targets* of intervention. They want to do something about them – they therefore have goals. The worker has to help the user choose goals that are limited, realistic and potentially achievable.

Users, as well as social workers also have ideas about what might be done to bring about the desired change –they identify *tasks*. 'The movement from problems to goals,' writes Marsh (2008: 122), 'takes place via tasks'. And finally, the worker sets *time-limits* to carry out the tasks.

Thus, says Marsh 'problems are *what is wrong* and the goals are *what is needed* . . .' (1991: 160 emphasis original). The tasks agreed and the order in which they are developed are the stepping stones that get users from problem to goal.

This idea of 'stepping stones' is one of the big plusses of task-centred work. Whenever we feel overwhelmed by our problems, there is a tendency to spin from one thing to another without ever getting to grips with matters. One way to tackle life's many demands, is to slow down the action, write lists of what needs to be done and in what order. We break problems down into manageable chunks and deal with them one at a time, systematically.

Commonsensical maybe, but this approach is the essence of task-centred work, and it has proved very effective when working with service users who feel anxious, overwhelmed and at sea.

If the approach is to be effective, the service user must want to do something about the problem. Motivation is key to success. Social workers must respect the ideas, indeed expertise that users often have about their own situation. Even though people have problems they also have strengths. It is these strengths that practitioners have to recognize and tap into. It is by working together on the task-centred enterprise that social workers form partnerships with their service users.

Task-centred social work is therefore highly structured. It certainly encourages clear thinking and forward planning. So, in the spirit of a task-centred approach, let's consider some of the key ideas in case order.

Problem exploration

This is a crucial stage. The service user considers and explores the nature, extent and significance of their problems. Similar to the techniques used in behaviour modification, it is important to help users describe their problems in clear, specific, and concrete detail. Ask how long it has been going on. Find out what the user has been trying to do about the problem.

For example, rather than simply accept a mother saying that she is 'stressed out and depressed' with the 'burden' of looking after her young disabled son, the social worker needs specific examples and the contexts in which they arise. The mother says that it takes a long time to prepare her son for school. She gets no help from her partner who sits watching television. The boy is getting physically bigger and sometimes she feels she just hasn't got the strength to handle him anymore. She feels that things can only get worse. She has tried shaming her partner into helping but this only leads to rows.

By the end of the problem exploration, both social worker and service user should have a clear, solid, explicit set of descriptions and characterizations of the major problems.

The final part of this stage is to put the problems in order of importance and urgency, *as perceived by the user*.

The problem exploration phase must not be skated over. In some cases it might even take several interviews. In any one episode of a task-centred intervention it is sensible to tackle only the one or two problems that are most pressing, and most amenable to resolution. Remember, success boosts confidence.

What is helpful about taking time over this stage is that it shows the service user that the problem has shape, it has boundaries, it has identifiable details. It isn't diffuse. It can be grasped. By giving the problem size, scope and specificity, there is the first hint that maybe it can be tackled. It isn't insurmountable. Perhaps it can be managed. This is a spur to the user.

Agreement

With a list of the main problems and their order of importance established, the worker and user agree which one or two problems will be the targets for change. Problems are typically classified as one of a number of recognizable types. These include such things as feeling dissatisfied in social relationships, experiencing conflict in personal relationships, inadequate resources, and behavioural problems.

It might be noted that the problems are not defined as ones of individual failure or weakness but rather ones of circumstance and situation. If you change the circumstance or situation (via actions and tasks), then you change the user's experience. Change is therefore achieved by focusing on the problem and not the person.

It is finally agreed that no more than, say 3 months, or 12 weekly sessions will be spent sorting out the problems. Brevity sharpens commitment. It focuses effort.

Tasks

When it's agreed what needs to change, some time is spent discussing what will help bring about the change. What tasks have to be carried out and by whom to achieve the goal are worked out. Goals are generally chosen because they are specific, achievable and easily described in behavioural terms.

For most people, *doing* things is more effective than thinking or talking about them. Changing the way you think and feel is often brought about by action. Task-centred work harnesses the user's potential for action, for doing things, not their proclivity to reflect and dwell.

The tasks identified are the result of negotiations between the worker and the user. Negotiation, says Marsh (2008: 122), is key to task-centred work. Negotiation establishes agreements and target problems, goals and tasks.

Tasks are not set by the worker for the user to carry out. Remember, task-centred work is collaborative. It's a partnership. The worker, or a third party, is just as likely as the service user to carry out an agreed task.

For example, the user might agree that by this time next week she will have contacted a local charity that runs a support group for parents of children who have a similar disability to that of her son. If possible she will request that she join the support group. For his part, the worker agrees to set up a meeting between the mother and her allegedly under-involved partner to discuss the situation and find ways forward. Depending on the outcome of this session, this task could lead to another involving couple counselling.

If a goal hasn't been reached or a task not carried out, this triggers further exploration. The approach allows for flexibility. Yes, it is structured and systematic, but it also demands that the worker is sensitive and responsive. If the task was to contact a marriage guidance counsellor but the user keeps saying she hasn't got round to it because the children's difficult behaviour has sapped all her energy, this 'clue' might signal the need for further exploration, a fresh negotiation and new task agreement. Marriage guidance counselling might be coming too early in the task sequence.

The task-centred approach is entirely comfortable using other methods such as counselling, short-term cognitive behavioural work or anger management so long as they further the overall resolution of the problem. The highly structured task-centred approach simply orchestrates the use of other skills and methods.

When they next meet a week later, worker and user review the success of the tasks they agreed to carry out. New tasks with new deadlines are then agreed, carried out and reviewed. And so on until the problem is resolved, always remembering that the absolute time-limit is roughly 3 months or less. Users expect change to be rapid and brisk when time-limits are set. Such expectations further increase motivation.

The method describes an incremental, step-by-step approach to changing problems. It is not expected that the completion of one task alone will see the user leap from problem to solution in one bound. To get from here (debt problem) to there (goal of being debt free), it may be necessary to get benefit forms, develop skills in completing them, visit a debt counsellor, prioritize the order in which debts get paid, and make an appointment to visit the housing department. These tasks can't all be done at once. They would overwhelm anyone. But broken down into manageable bits and tackled one at a time and in order, the chances of success rise.

Going from strength to strength

These are the bare bones of a task-centred approach. In practice, each stage has many refinements. As with all practices, a thorough knowledge of the theory and its methods leads to highly creative practices (Epstein and Brown 2002, Marsh and Doel 2005, Reid 2000).

But what is apparent, even from this sketch, is that task-centred work is positive and forward looking. No more agonizing about what deep psychological conflicts might underpin a user's problems. When people are encouraged to set about their difficulties in a clear, systematic, orderly and structured manner, it helps release previously unrecognized energy and potential.

Task-centred work can help users recover their confidence. They might be surprised to learn that they have abilities that are valued by others. They feel effective and worthwhile. It is well known that any technique that boosts a person's self-esteem and self-efficacy (both major resilience factors) is a good thing.

To a profession populated by people keen to help those in need, the pragmatism and optimism implied in task-centred work has proved very attractive. Task-centred work offers an early example of a practice that recognizes and taps into people's strengths. The concrete, time-limited and short-term nature of its practice made it instantly appealing to a profession used to long term interventions and 'deficit' models of human nature.

Thus, task-centred work seemed to usher in an era of solution-oriented and strengths-based approaches. Clearly these approaches were tuning into the mood of the time, almost as if there was something in the air. By the 1980s, the *zeitgeist* across much of the Western world was that everyone had it in them to make a difference, to achieve their goals. Only believe in yourself and you will achieve. Cast aside doubt. Accentuate the positive. Play to your strengths.

11

Be Responsible, Think Positive

Liberty and equality

The rise of task-centred work coincided with the rise of liberal market economics. Margaret Thatcher and Ronald Reagan were in the political ascendancy. Give people freedom and the right incentives and who knows what they might achieve, who knows how rich they might become.

Free market economies value, and reward, individuals who set about life with a go-getting, positive outlook. If you believe in yourself, everything is possible. Don't be negative. In the 1980s, a favourite management mantra of the day, already a cliché in its own time, was 'don't give me problems, bring me solutions'.

The rise of liberal economics and attempts to reclaim the virtues of personal responsibility were in part a reaction to decades of welfare politics in which the state and collective action were said to be suffocating freedom and individual choice. It was felt that the welfare state was making too many people dependent. It was discouraging initiative and responsibility. With its emphasis on fairness and equality, welfare politics had lost sight of the value of personal freedom.

It was acknowledged that the welfare state's origins and motives were honourable. Welfare politics and policy were themselves a late nineteenth century reaction to the unfettered freedom that on the one hand had driven the industrial revolution but on the other had created great poverty and misery. But maybe welfare thinking had gone too far.

What we had seen over the course of a century was a shift from the unqualified celebration of personal freedom in the early nineteenth century to a twentieth century awareness that if people are to live together in relative harmony, there needs to be some control. Total freedom leads to increasing inequality. And those with nothing might begin to feel they have nothing to lose, at which point they might threaten the social order. If left unchecked, such misery could be the undoing of the very social order that was supposed to support the free, independent individual (Howe 1996).

Therefore some shift in resources away from the rich to the poor becomes prudent. It wards off and dilutes social unrest. We also have the idea that if society is to be orderly and safe, the behaviour of its citizens needs to be the subject of some regulation. People can't be allowed to do just whatever they please. There needs to be some social discipline. But the emerging welfare state also had in its makeup and philosophy a more caring component. Within the bosom of welfare state provision, people were to be protected 'from the cradle to the grave.'

Social work, of course, is a product of the welfare state. Inextricably bound up with welfare theory and practice, by the 1980s social work was beginning to have a hard time at the hands of the new, buccaneering 'libertarians'. These 'neo-liberals' wanted to make people more free, more personally responsible and less dependent on welfare.

For too long, social workers and welfare politicians had argued that people weren't responsible for their woes. Rather, service users were the victims of broken homes, poverty and inequality. The 'neo-liberals', though, wanted no truck with this namby-pamby, do-good philosophy. Too much welfare thinking robbed people of their creative energy. Welfare concentrated on people's weaknesses and ignored their strengths. Too much social control and economic regulation was killing originality and productivity. The 'nanny state' may increase equality, but it takes away personal responsibility.

Welfare politics had been in the ascendancy since the Second World War. It was high time, argued the New Right libertarians, that the pendulum swung back to politics based on the concept of freedom and personal responsibility and away from politics based on equality and collective support. And this is what began to happen in the late 1970s and early 1980s.

It was felt that the welfare state had become too intrusive. It was sapping the moral fibre of its citizens. Social management had got out of hand. In spite of, or even because of the massive growth in welfare provision, crime rates were increasing, drug misuse was on the rise, and marriages were breaking down at alarming rates. As far as the New Right was concerned, in every sense the welfare state was not working. Freedom and the incentives that go with it were being stifled. The individual and individualism was being lost in a sea of mediocrity sponsored by increasing demands for equality.

The neo-liberals argued that a nation only prospers if it releases the entrepreneurial potential of its citizens. Personal liberty and a free-market economy are the way to set free this potential. Only when people are free – to think, to act, to be responsible – only then can individuals and economies unleash their creativity, realize their worth, and fulfil their ambitions.

Freedom versus welfare

In his analysis, Wagner (1994) recognized that modern times are made up of the two 'discourses' introduced above – one of freedom and one of equality. In the liberty camp are ideas such as freedom, justice and personal responsibility. In the equality camp are ideas such as fairness, welfare, social control, discipline and collective action designed to mitigate the worst excesses of the inequalities that total freedom tends to produce.

Although these two discourses co-exist, there is always political tension between them – freedom versus equality, individual liberty versus collective action, justice versus welfare, low taxes versus high taxes, unregulated markets versus statutory regulations to keep businesses in order.

The tension leads to a simple political division between those who argue for maximizing personal freedom ('the libertarians') and those who believe that if communities are to hold together and be of benefit to all, people must enjoy equal value and equal opportunity ('the communitarians'). Crudely speaking, the libertarians tend to be on the political right, while the communitarians occupy the political left. Those on the right want more freedom. Those on the left value social equality.

So across politics and the arts, economics and the social sciences, there was a shift from the political left to the political right, from welfare to justice. The individual and her strengths were re-discovered and celebrated. And something of this mood was clearly seeping into social work. As ever, social work was not only caught up in its times, to an extent it was changing in response to them (Harris develops this thought in his 2008 paper; also see Webb 2006).

For a century or more, social work had concerned itself with weakness and failure. Sometimes the failure was social; sometimes structural and economic. Here, radical social work might be the answer.

Or the weakness could be a moral or psychological flaw in the character of the individual. Problem behaviour might be the product of poor parenting or inappropriate learning. Emotional conflict could lead to mental ill health and rocky relationships. In these cases, psychodynamic casework or cognitive-behaviour therapy might be the social work answer.

Think positive

However, solution-focused and strengths-based social work turned matters on their head. In their analysis, even the problem-solving approaches start out with the wrong perspective. Beginning with an examination of the problem and not the solution is too negative. By the 1990s, social work was being courted by a growing number of these positivity promoting practitioners.

In response, many social workers began to revise the conceptual basis of their practice. They shifted from a viewpoint that started with people's weaknesses and deficits to one which valued their strengths and potential. It encouraged service users to feel responsible for carving out their own destinies. This was both exciting and empowering. Out of the window with psychodynamic casework and in with practices that celebrated people's inner strengths. The world is full of possibilities. The culture is one of 'can do'; solutions rather than problems.

Strengths-based, solution-focused, and 'possibility-thinking' social work were products of this change in the political climate. The approaches share an optimistic view of human nature. People have within them the answers to their own problems. Service users should be helped to discover and exploit their own strengths in order to achieve their goals. The role of the social worker was to help service users mobilize their own resources, to boost strengths and not treat weaknesses.

The service user as expert

Whereas psychodynamic, cognitive-behavioural, and radical approaches believe that expertise to explain what is going on and prescribe the answer lies with the practitioner, solutions and strengths perspectives credit the service user with the best knowledge and ultimate expertise about their problems and what to do about them.

Beckett helpfully highlights some of the differences between social work's traditional theories and the optimistic outlook of solutions and strengths perspectives:

> If we were to describe psychodynamic models as past-oriented and behaviourist approaches as more present-oriented, then [solution-focused, strengths perspectives and constructive social work] could perhaps be called *future*-oriented. (Beckett 2006: 65, emphasis original)

Thus, strengths-based approaches remained true to the liberal economic and individualistic political mood of the time:

> Asking clients to take responsibility for their own situation through their own problem solving is more helpful than trying to solve problems for them. (Simon 1994: 25)

Solution-focused and strengths-based techniques also had the virtue of being brief and potentially evidence-based. All of this was music to the ears of resource strapped, performance-driven social work managers. What could be better than a social work practice that was solution-focused, short-term and relatively easy to learn, at least in terms of its basic principles?

Mind your language

Perhaps more surprisingly, many of the underlying ideas that were supporting these positive practices were coming from some unexpected quarters. Interesting developments were taking place in psychology and social psychology, social construction theory and narrative theory, and even postmodernism. That's an intellectually high class line-up. Some of the key ideas common to the strengths-based perspectives, particularly those analyzing the way language shapes our experience, had their origins in these voguish disciplines.

We therefore need to consider what strengths and solution-focused approaches might have in common.

Language, particularly in the form of labelling, can all too easily define an individual. A label can determine how other people see us and how we experience ourselves. Much of our thinking is in words. Words carry meaning. And so the meaning we give to our own and other people's experience is affected by the language we use.

Goffman explored these ideas in a series of groundbreaking books including *Asylums: essays on the social situation of mental patients and other inmates* (1961) and *Stigma: notes on the management of spoiled identity* (1963). To label people in terms of an alleged deficit is to diminish them, to cast them as deficient, spoiled, incompetent.

It's all too easy to approach the 'mentally ill' or 'the dysfunctional family' with assumptions already in place about the nature of their deficiency or inadequacy. Those on the receiving end of labels that carry a stigma experience themselves as less than whole, less than normal, somehow 'spoiled'. Aware of the power of language to harm, practitioners began to learn new ways of talking. No longer was the talk of 'the mentally ill'. Rather it was to see people who just happened to have a mental illness.

More generally, solution-focused and strengths-based practitioners believe that language creates reality. The way people talk about themselves and their lives constructs their experience. Negative and fatalistic language creates negative and depressed realities. People who talk about problems often feel their life is more problematic. If their talk is positive, so will be their outlook on life. When these same people are encouraged to talk more about solutions, they feel that positive change really is possible.

> For example, if someone reports having a bad argument last night, we can wait for an opportunity to ask 'How did you end it?' Even if they can't tell how it was ended the question conveys that they were capable of ending it. When questions about solutions are asked consistently in a session the messages about the potential for change is more powerful still. (Parton and O'Byrne 2000: 57)

We begin to see that how people view and talk about their problem is inseparable from what they do about it (Eron and Lund 1993). Meaning and action, language and behaviour turn out to be intimately related.

The social construction of reality

In this perspective, there is no objective social reality. It is constructed by language and the meanings it carries at particular times and in certain places, in different societies and across various cultures. If you change the language, you change the meaning. If you change the meaning, you alter the individual's experience.

The aim therefore is to help users take control of the meaning of their own language and thereby change their experience, including the way they define and identify themselves. Female, black or disabled service users need to realize how so much of their experience is actually defined, and thereby constructed, by the prevailing ideological climate and the discourses it supports. Once they see this, they can free themselves from unhelpful labels, assumptions and expectations. Using a constructive social work approach helps service users talk about themselves, their reality and their experiences in new ways (Parton and O'Byrne 2000: 18). This can apply to a woman who is a victim of domestic violence, a black adolescent boy feeling alienated from school, or the prejudice experienced by a physically disabled employee in the work place.

Strengths, solutions and social constructive approaches are also supported by client experience studies. For many years, the message from service users has been the same. What they say is that in conversation with warm, interested and empathic social workers they value the chance to control the meaning of their own experience and the meaning that others give to that experience (Howe 1993: 195). It is when they recover feelings of personal control that service users begin to cope. Time now, then, to look at brief solution focussed and strengths-based perspectives in more detail.

12

Solution-focused Approaches

Be brief

Solution-focused therapy has its origins in brief family therapy (de Shazer 1985). Therapists at the Brief Family Therapy Center in Milwaukee noticed that many clients made progress even though they weren't dwelling or reflecting on the causes of their difficulties. Clients who talked about how they would like their lives to be different seemed to do well.

From the outset, solution-focused brief therapy (SFBT) starts with the expectation that treatment will not take long. Five or six sessions of no more than 45 minutes each is typical. There is also an expectation that problems or 'complaints' are easily resolved.

Change is normal. It is easy to achieve and the therapist fully expects the user and her situation to change for the better. This sets up a positive, change-oriented climate which is likely to be self-fulfilling. Change is constant. Expect change; change happens; change is inevitable. Learn to say: 'I would be surprised if you and your situation didn't change.' Solution-focused therapists, observes Murdock (2004: 207) 'are serious optimists.'

Key principles

Solution-focused therapy has a number of key principles (O'Hanlon and Weiner-Davis 1989, Murdock 2004: 408–11):

- Clients have resources and strengths to resolve complaints.
- Change is constant.
- The solution-focused therapist's job is to identify and amplify change.
- It is usually unnecessary to know a great deal about the complaint to resolve it.

- It is not necessary to know the cause or function of a complaint to resolve it.
- A small change is all that is necessary; a change in one part of the system can effect change in another part of the system.
- Solution-focused therapy is egalitarian.
- Clients define the goal.
- Rapid change or resolution of problems is possible.
- There is no one 'right' way to view things; different views may just be as valid and may fit the facts just as well.
- Focus on what is possible and changeable rather than on what is impossible and intractable.

The therapist helps shift users away from complaining about their difficulties. The focus is on what strengths they can bring to bear on the situation. The focus is also on things that have worked. The therapist finds out what users are already doing that is working, and then builds on it.

There is little or no interest in what has 'caused' the complaint or why the service user has the problem. It is not necessary to explain the cause of the problem to find a good solution. The question 'why' is rarely, if ever asked. Personal histories are of no interest. The focus is on sorting out the difficulty. The emphasis therefore is on client competence and strength, not deficit and pathology.

Users generally know what has to be done to achieve their goal, or if they have got stuck and their responses are simply not working, the therapist will help them do something different. We tend to carry on behaving in the same way when trying to deal with a problem even when clearly it isn't working. More of the same is rarely the answer. Shouting at a child, demanding to know why they misbehaved, only seems to make matters worse. And yet next time he is naughty, the parent shouts at the boy again. So what might happen if the parent ignores the boy? Or laughs? Or pulls a face? The therapist doesn't suggest the solutions. The user must come up with ideas themselves, choose one and then just see what happens.

Small positive changes are recommended to start with. These build confidence. They create a belief that change is possible. Goals therefore must be specific, concrete and attainable. Goals should also be recognized in terms of *doing* and *viewing* things differently.

Compliments and exceptions

Sometimes clients' lives are so hard-going that they can see no way out of their despair. 'One way forward,' suggests Iveson (2002: 150), 'is to be curious about how they cope – how they manage to hang on despite adversity'.

It is important to *compliment* clients on what they have managed to achieve and how they have been able to *cope* even under difficult circumstances. A good question to ask every time a service user either does something different or experiences a moment when the problem was absent is 'How did you do that?' This tips the conversation in a positive, solution-focused direction.

It is also the case that the user will experience times when the problem isn't present, when life, however fleetingly, was felt to be smooth-running. There is a great interest in these '*exceptions*'. The implication here is that there are times when whatever the user is doing, it is successful in keeping the problem at bay. So what is the user doing or thinking or feeling at such times? Perhaps she should do more of this kind of doing, thinking and feeling if it creates trouble-free experiences?

One of the key questions that gets the user into this positive mindset is '*When the problem is not present, how are things different?*' And then the therapist encourages the user to recover and stay in this mind-set.

For example, a social worker might ask 'When you felt less depressed yesterday, where were you, what were you doing, who were you with?' The implication is that the problem isn't always dominant or overwhelming. Too often, users over-generalize the problem and feel there is no escape, no light. Identifying exceptions gives the lie to the problem's inescapable all-pervasiveness.

Like many behaviourally oriented interventions, rather than use generalized terms, the user is asked to give concrete examples of what they mean. So what does a service user mean when he says he feels depressed? Stay in bed all day? Get stuck thinking over and over again about the pointlessness of life? Leave dishes unwashed in the sink for days?

The trick here is to stay in the trouble-free state of mind and stop dwelling on the problem. For example, the therapist might ask: 'What is it like when you are not feeling anxious?' Or, 'Tell me what you did the time when your partner didn't respond sarcastically.' Recognizing, exploring and appreciating these 'exceptions' and using them to find solutions is an important task. Often simply not thinking about the problem is half the battle.

The miracle question

Solution-focused brief therapy is perhaps best known for its use of the *miracle question*: 'Suppose that one night, while you are asleep, a miracle happened and the problem was solved. How would you know? What would be different?'

In effect the service user is being invited to come up with solutions. It also requires them to look to the future, to consider what life will actually look and feel like when the problem isn't there. The question is designed to de-rail them. They are forced out of the current problem groove in which they have become stuck. The question jumps them onto a new set of tracks that are going somewhere more positive and purposeful. This is how de Shazer (1985: 5) asked the question:

> Now, I want to ask you a strange question. Suppose that while you are asleep tonight and the entire house is quiet, a miracle happens. The miracle is that the problem which brought you here is solved. However, because you are sleeping, you don't know that the miracle has happened. So, when you wake up tomorrow morning, what will be different that will tell you that a miracle has happened and the problem that brought you here has been solved?

The question encourages the client to give a concrete description of how the world will be different. The more tangible the description, the more the client can grasp what needs to be done. The solution is now in sight.

A question of scale

Scaling questions aim to make the problem specific and concrete. The client is asked to rate the problem on a scale of 0 to 10, with 0 being the problem at its worst and 10 is the score when the problem has been solved. The client is then asked 'What one or two things could you do this week to raise the score by one or two points?' Whatever the client suggests can then be set as *homework*.

So, at the end of each session, the therapist and user agree a solution-relevant task – a form of homework – to be tried or completed before the next meeting.

The next session begins with a review of the homework task. If there was positive change and good things happened, the therapist will ask 'How did the change make your day go differently?' She may ask 'What's better?' These small, incremental steps boost confidence.

> The task will usually fall into one of two categories: behavioural or observational (De Jong and Berg 2002). With a behavioral task, the practitioner suggests that the client do more of those things that were identified as parts of the positive exceptions that occurred in the past . . . Observational tasks ask clients to become more observant of those times when the problem is less of a problem or not a problem at all – in other words exceptions. The main point is to help the client become more aware of those times when the problem is better . . . The more clearly the client has defined his or her goal, the easier it is to formulate a task. (Boyle et al 2006: 246)

The following treatment, which also offers a good example of scaling, optimism, being positive and being solution-minded, is taken from O'Connell's (2005: 56) very practical and readable introduction to solution-focused therapy:

Counsellor: On a scale of zero to ten, ten being you would do anything to overcome these panic attacks and zero being you would really love to but you don't think you will do anything, where would you put yourself today?

Client: Three.

Counsellor: Will three be good enough to make a start?

Client: No. I feel I've tried everything and nothing works. I've almost given up hope that it could get any better.

Counsellor: So although you've had a lot of set-backs you've managed to keep trying? Some people would have completely given up. How have you kept going?

Client: We've always been fighters in my family. My mum taught me to keep at it when things weren't going well.

Counsellor: So if she was here she would say keep fighting?

Client: Yes.

Counsellor:	Where would you need to get to on the scale before you felt you had a chance of fighting off the panic attacks?
Client:	Five.
Counsellor:	How will you know when you've got to five?
Client:	If I could relax more. I feel so tense most of the time, it keeps giving me headaches and then I feel like giving up.
Counsellor:	How would you go about being relaxed enough to feel you were getting to five?
Client:	I don't know.
Counsellor:	When the sun comes out for you and you feel less tense than usual what has helped to make you better?
Client:	When I am on my own and I can listen to my own music.
Counsellor:	Anything else?
Client:	I like Fridays when I don't have to go to work. I can lie in and potter around a bit.
Counsellor:	Does this mean that if this Friday you put on your music and had an easy start to the day, you'd possibly feel a five and more able to fight back against the panic attacks?
Client:	I think so.
Counsellor:	If you're a three today, what would help to get you to be a four?

These techniques are just a few of the many developed by solution-focused practitioners. There are fast-forward questions ('Look at yourself in the future when the problem no longer exists').

There are surprise tasks ('Do at least one or two things that will surprise your partner, child, father etc. Don't tell them what it is. See if they can spot the difference. See if they react differently').

Whatever the technique, it will be apparent that solution-focused therapists are constantly encouraging the service user to see themselves as problem-free. Having imagined the future, the user is then asked to describe how she got there, what did she do? So why not try it? You had the answers all along. You have it in you. Do it!

Present tense, future perfect

Although there is not a lot of robust, well-designed research to say whether or not solution-focused approaches are more effective than other therapies (Murdock 2004: 428), there is an undeniable positive

So, if you can help people change the way they use language to describe and think about themselves so that it is altogether more positive and optimistic, first their reality will change and then their behaviour. In effect, the service user's reality is reconstructed simply by changing the quality and direction of language used. As the service user and practitioner communicate, users create new ways of viewing their lives. Solutions to problems are shaped by worker and user within a positive, more optimistic language environment.

Constructive social work creatively mixes solution-focused and narrative therapies with one of sociology's major theoretical perspectives, the social construction of reality. Task-centred, solution-focused and constructive social work all agree that social work should play to service users' strengths. Dennis Saleebey and his colleagues took them at their word.

13

The Strengths Perspective

Label with care

We have seen that because language carries meaning, there is an insistence by solutions and strengths-based practitioners to attend to the way language is used. Who has slapped this label on you? What does the label signify? Is this the way you think about yourself? Can you cast aside the label and all that it implies and regain control over what actually it means to be you?

Strengths-based social work insists that those with whom we work are far more than the labels society confers on them. All too often, entry into the health and social services requires that a label is first applied. 'Consequently,' writes Witkin (2002: xiii), 'it is hard to see the person with mental illness or the child abuser as something other than their labels . . . Negative situations seem to cry out for negative explanations – we want to know what is wrong when so little seems right.'

Strengths perspectives not only demand that we see the person behind the label, but that we also recognize that the individual has potential, has strengths, and it is this potential and these strengths that must be recognized, acknowledged and released.

Resilience and resourcefulness

Strengths-based social work began to take shape in the late 1980s. There was a feeling in some circles that for too long social workers had concentrated on service users' deficiencies – social work was deficit-oriented (Weick et al 1989). Too many social work practices saw service users as victims, either of their own histories, psychologies, or place in the social structure. These approaches de-valued clients and demoralized social workers. It was all too easy for service users to buy into this pathological, deficit model of themselves. Social workers therefore had to challenge mind-sets that saw the self as victim.

Saleebey, one of the founders of the strengths-based approach, felt increasingly unconvinced by practices that concentrated on people's pathology and problems. Over the years, he argues, the medical model has played far too big a part in social work's thinking and practice.

The strengths perspective began to recognize and value the *resilience* and *resourcefulness* possessed by many people living in adversity. Moreover, practices based on people's strengths seemed to sit very comfortably with social work's values. Strengths and solution-focused therapies pride themselves on being egalitarian. Social workers should believe in people and their strengths. Service users should be respected. They should be *empowered*. They should enjoy self-determination. Life is full of possibility and promise.

Resilience is the concept that psychologists use to describe people's ability to deal competently with risk, to overcome hazards, to continue functioning well under pressure. Many attributes predict increased resilience: humour; optimistic temperament; good self-esteem; planfulness; emotional intelligence.

But one of the most valuable resiliences is the ability to find, sustain and enjoy good quality relationships. In other words, although many resilience factors are characteristics of the individual, just as important is the quality of people's social supports and relationships. Relationships are where we enjoy love and care, esteem and recognition. Other people can be sources of information, advice and support. There is pleasure and comfort in friendship.

If good relationships do boost resilience, and resilience allows people to play to their strengths, social workers need to be very mindful of the quality and extent of service users' interpersonal lives. Problem-solving, healing and 'self-righting' nearly always take place in the context of supportive relationships. Goldstein (2002) quotes the work of Jordan (1992) to make the same important point:

> Resilience, in her terms is a relational dynamic nurtured by a two-way process of mutuality and empathy – a process of 'sharing with' more so than 'getting from'. (p 32)

Far more than social workers realize, service users can and do bounce back. Most of us seem to have 'self-righting' instincts. We strive to put our lives back in order, straighten ourselves out. When we consider the stresses under which many service users live, we have to be impressed with their ability to keep going, perhaps not all of the time, but more often than we give them credit.

Drawing on your strengths

It is the times when the service user keeps going in the face of adversity in which the strengths-based worker is particularly interested. The social worker wants to tease out and recognize what strengths, talents, experience, skills, resources and supports the service user was drawing on to cope with the stress.

After being abandoned by her partner, what did a mother do to keep out of debt and yet still manage to feed the children? Although currently feeling depressed at her failure to get a job, what is it about a young woman with learning difficulties that enables her to maintain a close and caring set of friends? It is these strengths that have to be applauded. It is these strengths that have to be supported. Talents and skills such as these have to be boosted.

> First and foremost, the strengths perspective is about discerning those resources, and respecting them and the potential they may have reversing misfortune, countering illness, easing pain, and reaching goals. To detect strengths, however, the social work practitioner must be genuinely interested in, and respectful of, clients' stories, narratives, and accounts – the interpretive slants they take on their own experiences . . . clients want to know that you believe they can surmount adversity and begin to climb towards transformation and growth. (Saleebey 2002: 14)

Listening to and being interested in people's stories is a very effective way of finding out what are people's strengths. Saleebey gives the example of Bill, a man in his early forties who had been in and out of hospital with a variety of mental illnesses including a diagnosis:

> Bill . . . was assigned a first-year MSW student as a case manager . . . She began by encouraging Bill to 'tell his stories' – how he got to be where he was, what interesting things he had done, and how he had survived with a serious illness. She learned many interesting things about Bill, and some of his stories clearly revealed a resourceful, motivated person. (Saleebey 2002: 88)

The social worker can also discover people's strengths by asking certain kinds of question. Saleebey (2002: 89) identifies a number of these.

- *Survival questions* ask users about who has helped them in the past. Who has offered support, given advice. The user is asked how they came across these people and why they think they chose to give help.
- *Exception questions* invite service users to wonder what was happening when things were going well. What were they doing on the occasion when they did feel on top of things?
- *Possibility questions* ask users about their hopes. Service users are asked 'Which people and what personal qualities are helping you move in the hoped for directions?
- *Esteem questions* include asking 'When people say good things about you, what are they likely to say? What is it about you and your life that have given you real pride and pleasure?'

It is apparent from these questions that the strengths-based practitioner is constantly helping people recognize and embrace those good, successful, valued bits of themselves. These bits might appear few, but it is on these solid, positive elements of self that success will be built.

'There is often great resistance,' observes Saleebey (2002: 90), 'to acknowledging one's competence, reserves and resourcefulness. In addition, many traits and capacities that are signs of strength are hidden under the rubble of years of self-doubt, the blame of others, and, in some cases, the wearing of a diagnostic label'.

The expert self

The social worker has to believe in people's innate capacity to do something about their lives. Living with their problems and worries day in day out, service users tend to know their problem better than anyone else. 'What they have not been able to do,' write Weick and Chamberlain (2002: 98), 'is find a way to get past the problem. The task of the social worker is to help people to get past the problem'. This is why social workers encourage story telling, ask questions about successes, listen carefully, believe, and ask about hopes for the future. Out of these interactions, the user begins to recognize and believe in themselves and their strengths.

Everyone, if given the chance, has ideas about how life could be better. Service users have a surprising amount of knowledge and expertise about their lives, their relationships and how to survive, often in dire circumstances. If they are encouraged and supported, service users, individually and collectively, have the capacity to bring about change.

> Mobilize clients' strengths (talents, knowledge, capacities) in the service of achieving their goals and visions and the clients will have a better quality of life on their terms. (Saleebey 1997: 4)

The approach is forward looking. It explores future *possibilities*. When faced with a problem, individuals are instinctively driven to do something about it, to 'self-heal'. They know what is in their interest and they know what their interests are. Social workers don't. To know better than the other what is the matter and what he should do about it is to devalue him.

Building on success

However, the meanings that people give to experience can get stuck. They become trapped in a negative or unhelpful language 'frame'. They lose sight of possibilities. Help aims to get people to use different words and see new meanings. A change of language can lead to a change of response. In this way, clients are helped to move from a 'problem frame' to a 'possibility frame'.

Summarizing the work of Saleebey (1997) and others, Healy (2006: 158–64) describes five practice principles.:

- Adopt an optimistic attitude;
- Focus primarily on assets;
- Collaborate with the service user;
- Work towards the long-term empowerment of service users; and
- Create community – link service users to others to promote self-help communities.

The approach constantly demands that social workers seek out service users' capacities. 'Every individual, group, family, and community has strengths' (Saleebey 1997: 12). These can include what people have learned about themselves, their virtues, the world in which they live, their previous ways of coping, their past successes, and their talents. Any success must be recognized by the social worker. There must be *compliments*.

> I know you're feeling very distressed, but I must say I'm impressed that you're here, on time. You clearly want to do something about your situation. That's excellent.

For those who think that the strengths perspective is just a new way of packaging traditional social work values of 'building on clients strengths' and 'start where the client is', Saleebey says think again:

> . . . let us be clear: The strengths perspective is a dramatic depart-ure from conventional social work practice. Practicing from a strengths orientation means this – everything you do as a social worker will be predicated, in some way, on helping to discover and embellish, explore and exploit clients' strengths and resources in the service of assisting them to achieve their goals, realize their dreams, and shed the irons of their own inhibitions and misgiv-ings, and society's domination. (Saleeby 2002: 1)

Even when people have struggled, say with a housing problem or car-ing for a husband with Alzheimer's Disease, they will have shown some strengths. The worker might begin by acknowledging the strength required simply to have kept going:

> I know it's been extremely hard, but I must admit I'm impressed with what you've managed to do so far. What skills, what strengths have helped you to keep going?

> What are you doing that helps reduce your anxiety?

> Given what you've been through, how have you managed to cope and fight against the odds?

People are encouraged to see that they are more than their problem. Everyone can be resourceful when pursuing their own interests. Users will have ideas about who might be available to help or advise, or what benefits might be tapped. A worker might ask a father directly what strengths he has and how these might be used to fulfil his family's hopes.

We can only build on strengths. Talk of weakness is to build the house on sand. The case will collapse. Despair will increase. It is the solid bits of the user's life to which we must attend. What skills do they have? What knowledge? What successes? What insights? What do they think is going on and why? What do they think might move matters on and make a difference? These are the strengths of the situation. That is where future success lies. That's where we must build. For example:

> . . . let's say we are working in a school context and a young person is referred to us because of their absenteeism. The referral from the school principal tells us that, on average, the young person misses two days of school per week. From a strengths perspective we would not focus on the two days missed per week, but rather, we turn our attention to what keeps the young person at school three days per week. Moreover, using a strengths perspective approach to listening we would seek out strengths, not only within the individual, but also within their formal and informal networks. So we could ask the young person: 'Tell me about someone who wouldn't be surprised to know that you had managed to get yourself to school three days per week despite everything that is going on for you.' (Healy 2005: 159–60)

Stepping back, we have noted that the emergence of the strengths approach reflects the broader societal shift from a problem-based to solution-focused outlook. The emphasis is no longer on individual deficiency but personal responsibility. Although several generations down the line, strengths based social work is clearly a close cousin of Octavia Hill's and Charles Loch's approach to social work. They challenged their clients to be independent and hard working. You can certainly see the family resemblance.

Up until the 1960s social work tended to be past-oriented. In contrast in the 1990s social work became forward looking. In all of these respects strengths-based social work shares much common ground with brief solution-focused brief therapy, constructive social work and task-centred work.

If we tease out the key words that these have approaches have in common we see further evidence that they are a product of their times. Solutions, strengths, possibilities, future-oriented, and forward looking – they all chime well with a liberal, personal responsibility, creative, self-defining agenda. These approaches have re-charged many areas of social work.

Strength in numbers

Minds, as well as bodies, have a remarkable capacity to self-heal. Personal resilience can be bolstered by recognizing personal strengths but it can also be enhanced by working together with others who share the same needs and experiences. Not only does meeting others generate ideas, it helps people believe in themselves.

Other people can be a source of support and change, particularly when group members share the same kind of need or problem. When people are brought together, a creative force is unleashed. Possibilities are recognized. When communities share the same interest they become energized and motivated. Knowing you are not alone is both a comfort and an incentive.

If they believe in themselves and have energy and conviction, individuals working together can drive change. They have the power. If a much valued day care centre for old people is threatened with closure, challenge that decision. If a children's playground is run-down and an eye-sore, plan its improvement.

The community and the people in it are the major asset. A strengths-based, asset-oriented approach can be used to great effect by town planners, community development workers, and group workers. Communities can be defined by geography (everyone who lives in a run-down part of town) or need (young single mothers or people with Down's syndrome).

And within and around any community, however defined, will be a number of interested groups and organizations. Schools, businesses, neighbourhood groups, voluntary organizations, local government agencies and self-help groups are all potential assets. When they are brought together, they can connect. Together they can recognize needs, pool strengths, identify solutions and bring about change.

However, there are a group of theories that have taken this wider perspective even further. They have sought to integrate and unify social work's interest in service users as individuals, families, groups and even whole communities. They see links between each of these levels of interest. Their aim is to see social work and what it does as a seamless web of interconnected activity. The tool that they use to knit all of this diverse thinking together is systems theory.

14

Systemic and Ecological Approaches

Interconnected and interdependent

Our relationships with each other are forever being shaped and re-shaped by our mutual interactions. We affect and are affected by each other. On the larger stage, we also change in response to shifts in the economy, the political environment, technology, the outpourings of the media, and the pressure of social and class forces. We inhabit a busy, interconnected world of people, things, ideas and events.

Ecologists are scientists who study the complexities of this social matrix. They study the interconnectedness and inter-relatedness of people and the world in which they live.

In the original, Oxford English Dictionary definition, *ecology* refers to that branch of biology that deals with the way plants and animals relate with one another and to the physical environment in which they live.

Modern worries about climate change are a good example of how the biological world and the physical world are intimately related. For example, if you increase carbon dioxide and methane in the atmosphere, more of the sun's heat is retained by the Earth. Just like a greenhouse, these gases trap heat – hence they are known as greenhouse gases.

However, if you heat up the atmosphere, you will cause ice at the poles to melt, sea level to rise, and the oceans to warm up. Plankton that thrives in cold seas dies off. Krill and fish that feed off the plankton begin to starve. The sea birds that live off the fish find their food source disappearing and so their numbers fall. The bird droppings that fertilized the thin, rocky soil on which they built their nests are no longer deposited. What little vegetation there was on the thin soil depended on the nutriments provided by the bird droppings.

The small mouse that lived off the grasses and tiny plants has nothing to eat so it becomes extinct along with the foxes that hunted the mice.

You get the idea. We could continue this account of how one thing affects another in a never-ending series of consequences, but you see why the study of ecological systems is interesting, slightly mind-blowing, and to an extent unpredictable. Change one thing and you end up changing other things that are totally unexpected.

Ecology can also be used as a science to think about people's interactions with their environment. For human beings, this environment includes not only things but even more importantly other people.

General systems theory

Social workers have always had an interest in the big picture. There are many ways to trace the history of this big picture thinking, but perhaps the simplest route in is to begin with systems theory and work towards modern ecological models as they have been employed by social workers.

Our individual and collective behaviour is influenced by everything from our genes to the political environment. It is not possible to fully understand our development and behaviour without taking into account all of these elements. And indeed, this is what some social work theories insist that we do if we are to make effective interventions.

Lying behind these models is the idea that everything is connected, everything can affect everything else. Complex systems are made up of many parts. It is not possible to understand the whole without recognizing how the component parts interact, affect and change each other. As the parts interact, they create the character and function of the whole.

This description amounts to a definition, albeit a simplistic one, of general systems theory. The usual example to give at this point is the humble thermostat and central heating system.

The thermostat measures the room's temperature. It is connected to a boiler that heats water. The hot water is pumped to radiators that when hot warm up the room. If the room temperature is too low, the thermostat senses the drop in heat. It sends an electrical signal to the boiler to switch itself on. This heats up the water which is sent to the radiator that warms up the room. When the room reaches the right temperature, the thermostat senses the change. It then sends a second signal back to the boiler to switch itself off. The radiator cools and so does the room. This 'feedback' cycle gets repeated again and again so that in effect the room stays at more or less a constant temperature. Keeping a system such as room temperature in a constant state is known as 'homeostasis.'

The same idea can be applied to biological organisms or systems. Hearts, lungs, blood vessels, stomachs, guts, muscles, kidneys, livers, and nerve cell all function to keep the whole body system functioning. Every part communicates with and is affected by every other part. If one part goes wrong, it has a serious knock-on effect. And if the body is yours, you start to feel ill.

For example, if the liver fails, the body can no longer store glucose. Glucose releases energy. Therefore if you can't store glucose, you tire very easily. You have no energy. If your liver begins to fail, you also suffer problems with the way your nervous system functions. Amino acid breakdown and removal of nitrogen and other foreign material from your body also begin to pack up. These toxins build up and slowly poison you. By this stage you are definitely feeling unwell.

So whatever the illness, medical treatments are attempts to treat those parts of the body's system that are failing. The aim is to bring the individual back to health, back to homeostatis.

The pioneer of general systems theory, Ludwig von Bertalanffy (1968), first applied his ideas to biological systems. But he also began to see the relevance of his theory to social systems and even individual psychological states.

The family as a system and family therapy

Some of the earliest social science enthusiasts to use these ideas were family therapists (for example, Minuchin 1974, Satir 1967). They saw the family as a system. Parents and children interact and are in constant communication. What one family member thinks, feels, says or does affects what other family members think, feel, say and do. Often these interactions circulate in a complex fashion around the family system. To appreciate family life, you have to look simultaneously at both the individual and the family.

Here's another simple, standard example. A teenage daughter stays out late at night because she says her father is 'always on at' her.

He says he 'goes on at' her because she stays out late at night and he worries about her safety. The circular logic of these behaviours can only be changed if either one or both parties agree to alter their behaviour. This is classic family therapy territory.

Family therapists don't accept that any individual family member is at fault. Problems are best understood at the level of the family. Family life is a system of interacting parts. Therefore the whole family has to be seen and 'treated' if change is to happen. Blaming an individual is merely making them a scapegoat. Invariably, whenever there is a problem in a family, it's better to look at the whole rather than the parts.

When thinking about a system, including a family system it is helpful think of each part, each family member in dynamic relationship with every other part or family member. There is interdependence. Rather than think about what is taking place at the individual level, consider what is happening *between* people. Think *interpersonally*, not intrapsychically. Think *here-and-now* rather than past-and-then.

Family therapists believe that open systems are more healthy than closed systems. Open systems are much better at adapting to new situations and changing environments. For example, people with closed minds are rigid and often at odds with other people. In contrast, open-minded people are more interested in what goes on around them. They are open to new ideas. They evolve, adapt and move with the times. They are more tolerant.

The same ideas apply to families. Families are in a constant state of change and flux. Children grow older and get ideas of their own. Members leave or die. New members arrive through birth and marriage. Closed families do not cope well with these changes. As they struggle, tensions arise and problems appear. The teenage son who refuses to join the family on a day out gets into an argument with his father. The boy's increasingly moody and awkward behaviour is seen as a problem. He has to fit in with the family's fixed routines. The family doesn't evolve. His parents see him as the problem and it is their son who must change.

Open families adapt well to change. Relationships are constantly being re-configured. Healthy families allow members to grow, evolve and achieve autonomy which paradoxically keeps the family close, united and happy. They show respect for each other. There is give-and-take. The aim of family therapists is therefore to help 'stuck' families to loosen up. It is only then that they can move on.

In pursuit of helping families develop more open, relaxed, attuned relationships both with each other and the outside world, family therapists have developed a wonderful array of concepts and techniques many of which have been very influential in social work (for example, see Burnham 1986, Carr 2000, Dallos and Draper 2000, Walker and Akister 2005, White 2008).

No-blame, no-shame, re-frame

Families might learn not to blame just one individual member for all their woes. Therapists foster a climate of 'no-blame'. They help families to 're-frame' the problem. For example, a Mum's anger with her daughter is re-cast as an expression of concern, albeit a very agitated concern. The daughter's increasingly disengaged attitude is presented as a way of not making matters worse; her presence only seems to make Mum more upset, so she keeps out of the way. Helping families appreciate this alternative way of seeing things is half the battle.

People tend to behave in the ways that they do for a reason and it's often helpful to understand these reasons. But it is often very difficult for families to recognize, listen and become aware of what each other is thinking and feeling. Somehow, the family therapist has to get so much of this unspoken, unrecognized information out into the open.

Therapists also use similar 're-framing' techniques to help families understand why it's best to work together. A practitioner might say:

> It's good that you've all turned up to-day. Many families would have fallen apart and given up. We often find that problems of this kind are resolved more quickly when everyone is involved. This way we get everyone's point of view and lots of ideas about how we might sort things out.

Thinking systemically

Although the above offers only the briefest snapshot of family therapy, nevertheless the outline indicates the potential value of thinking 'systemically'. Problems rarely have a single, straightforward cause. It's often better to see things in the round, from different perspectives.

Analyzing situations using systems theory often throws up surprises and unexpected solutions. Here is an uplifting example, with distinct cognitive-behavioural overtones played out in a family systemic arena:

A young girl seemed to be developing agoraphobia. She rarely left the house. Her school attendance plummeted. During extensive reflective and exploratory work with the girl, her mother, father and maternal grandmother the following explanation (and solution) emerged.

The mother had suffered a very poor school experience herself. She never learned to read or write. Taking her daughter to the school gates each morning made the mother increasingly anxious and distressed as memories of failure and ridicule uncontrollably flooded into her mind. The daughter sensed that her mother was behaving more and more oddly on the way to school which she found frightening. She dealt with this by refusing to go to school. This meant that her mother didn't get upset and the little girl didn't feel frightened.

The creative solution worked out very carefully and with great sensitivity by the social worker was to encourage the mother to attend adult-literacy classes where she learned to read and write. Her husband agreed to support her in this task. The mother's confidence rocketed and it wasn't long before she had no problems taking her daughter to school. Indeed, she eventually met her daughter's teacher, talked about her own literacy problems and how these had inadvertently affected the girl.

Knowing that Mum could now read and write, the teacher wondered if the mother would like to come into school one morning a week and listen to some of the younger children read, particularly those who were struggling. Mum, after some anxious hesitation, agreed, and never looked back.

Given the complex world of people in relationship with other people and their environment, it's obvious why social work has always been fascinated by systems-based thinking and practice. What's interesting is how this fascination expresses itself in so many different ways. It's as if each generation of social workers has to discover for itself the rich interconnectedness that links people and their environment.

The person-in-their-environment

The 1960s and early 1970s saw a productive marriage of psychodynamic theory and a systemic way of thinking. It was often referred to as a psychosocial approach in which the person was seen to be in constant interaction with her environment, particularly her social environment of family, friends, neighbours, health and social care workers. The idea that people can only be fully understood in relationship to their environment almost defines social work.

If people are both psychological beings and social entities, it seems natural to employ a psychosocial, person-environment, individual-society approach, all set within a systems framework. By the late 1960s, this is what many social work theorists were beginning to do.

The most well-known exponent of the psychosocial approach was Florence Hollis (1964, 1972) who talked of the 'person-situation gestalt' as central to her mode of practice.

> We know that the individual is in constant interaction – or transaction – with other members of his immediate family; with other relatives; with a network of friends and acquaintances, including neighbors, with an employer if he works; and so on through all his social relationships … The unit of attention in casework becomes those systems that appear to be of salient importance to the problem for which the individual has sought help or to others that later become the focus of treatment. A primary characteristic of any system is that all parts of a system are in transaction, so that whatever affects one part of the system affects all parts to some degree. (Hollis 1972: 10–11)

Psychosocial casework was to the fore in social work throughout much of the 1960s. But a new breed of systems theory enthusiasts burst onto the social work scene in the 1970s. They generated complex models of social work in which everyone and everything was linked to and was affected by everyone and everything else in the service user's life. There has always been a strong urge in social work to pull all the component bits of the profession together into some all-encompassing whole. So why not see all of social work's skills, methods and knowledge based on a platform of shared purposes and values?

Unitary approaches

To capture the wholeness of social work, this new generation of systems theorists described their social work models and the approaches they sponsored as 'unitary' and 'integrated'. The search was on for social work's common base (Bartlett 1970).

For example, a husband who was rejected as a child frequently gets into violent arguments with his wife. These arguments upset the children, particularly the 9-year-old boy who has learning difficulties. He often runs away to his maternal grandmother but she is getting old. His upset distresses her. A recent illness meant that she had to be admitted to hospital. The next time the little boy ran away and truanted from school, he had nowhere to go, and so he slept in a derelict house.

There's clearly a lot going on this case. Three generations are involved. Individuals, couples and families are affected. The school and the hospital have expressed worries. Where would you start? With the father's temper? With the married couple or the family? With the 9-year-old boy? Should the focus be on the father's unresolved feelings about his childhood rejection? Could you change the parents' behaviour? Could the boy's school have a useful role to play?

When you start thinking in this wide ranging way, it dawns on you that each part affects the whole. It may therefore be helpful to start thinking about the whole 'system'.

These complex models have intellectual appeal. After all, who could disagree that poor housing increases people's levels of stress and that stressed people are more likely to argue and have relationship problems. Relationship problems reduce levels of social support and poor support increases the risk of mental health and behavioural problems. People with behavioural problems find it difficult to cope with work. Unemployment leads to poverty, which adds to stress and family problems. Where do you start with this sorry circular chain of events?

Systemically speaking, it simply won't do to think about needs and problems at the level of the individual. Social workers have to consider the wider context. We live in a social web. Tug one thread and vibrations ripple out in all directions.

Here is Max Siporin making the case in his 1975 book for an integrated view of social work:

> ... the profession of social work has been seeking a single vision of its mission, of its knowledge and methodology. In our pluralistic society such a quest may seem unrealistic, but it is necessary for social work effectiveness as a helping profession that there be some common identity, in a shared core of purpose, philosophy, knowledge and method ... this book ... articulates a generic framework for the scientific practice of social work as a whole. It offers bridges between social work clinical and therapeutic orientations and activities and those of community planning, social policy and administration, and social action ... This book also gives expression to the still emergent configurations of theory and method, which transcend older conceptions of practice in terms of casework, group work, or community organization. (Siporin 1975: vii)

Well, that's a worthy but very ambitious vision. Siporin's book is a scholarly attempt to bring together all of social work's major theories, methods and values. Similar unifying projects using a systems theory perspective were attempted by Goldstein 1973, Pincus and Minahan 1973, Meyer 1976, Davies 1977, and Specht and Vickery 1977. The expanded vision of social work offered by these writers left social workers wide-eyed. It was also in danger of leaving them daunted.

Systems breakdown

Looking back, it seems that the 1970s was a decade in which social work witnessed many attempts to join everything up, intellectually, organizationally and professionally. There was much coming together and big-picture thinking. Systems theory provided an elegant conceptual framework in which to place this generic social work vision.

In England and Wales, 1971 saw the formation of Social Services Departments that brought together previously separate children, mental health, welfare and medical social work departments. Social workers no longer specialized in work with children or older people or mental illness. They worked generically.

A typical day in the mid-1970s would see a social worker first thing in the morning visit an old woman suffering dementia, take a child abuse referral before lunch, and then spend the afternoon sorting out home aids and adaptations for a man suffering severe arthritis. And all of this generic practice was set within the unitary, integrated, systems theory-based models of social work. There was a lot to think about and get your head round. For front-line practitioners, it really was too much.

It seemed only a matter of time before there would be a return to specialist social workers and a retreat from some of the more extravagant ambitions of an all-embracing model of social work. Knowledge and skills were being spread too thin. Jacks and Jills of all trades were in danger of being masters and mistresses of none.

Although able to appreciate the conceptual elegance of these unitary approaches, many social workers gradually returned to less generic, more specialist forms of practice. A practitioner might find herself working with adults with a mental illness using task-centred and cognitive-behavioural approaches, perhaps with some occasional group work. Another, concentrating on working with older and frail people, finds that person-centred and anti-discriminatory perspectives generally suited his philosophy and value base.

Slowly, the unitary approach fragmented, at least at the level of individual practice. And maybe this was always the intention of the grand visionaries. Social work was all of the things that they said composed its make up – therapeutic casework to community development. But although the big picture was a true description of social work, it was made up of lots of individual, more specialist practices. It was only when you stepped back that you could see the ecological landscape appear in its full richness.

Interdisciplinarity seemed the way forward. Collaboration, communication and cooperation between caseworkers and community development specialists, family and mental health workers, therapists and rights advocates defines the totality of the social work enterprise, but no one practitioner could possibly be expected to grasp, never mind develop generic expertise at the unitary level.

The need to work with others, across disciplines and across professions is the only realistic way to address the complexity and interconnectedness that describes the service user's experience as defined by the ecological perspective. So although the whole is still the level at which to appreciate the service user's life, in practice, individual social workers and social care workers can only do justice to the grand picture by working at an interdisciplinary level. The ambition is no longer to create generic, all-singing, all-dancing social workers but specialists who work together in a 'joined-up', integrated, interdisciplinary whole.

Ecological models

Ecological thinking still attracts social workers. The ecological perspective is so dominant and powerful in modern day biology, developmental psychology and the environmental sciences that it is bound to attract social work theorists. People grow, mature and develop physically and psychologically from infancy to adulthood. And people live in busy, complex physical, psychosocial, political and economic environments. It would be remiss of social workers not to be aware of the ecological context in which they practice.

An ecologist who has been particularly influential on social work theory and practice is Urie Bronfenbrenner, a Russian born, American-based developmental psychologist.

Bronfenbrenner (1979) saw how people's lives were affected by both things close to home and further away. Our genetic make-up affects our temperament, personality, intelligence and many of our behavioural traits. Genes interact with their environment. Family and friends clearly have an impact on experience and development. But the climate in which we live our lives, indeed the very way we think, is also affected by the neighbourhoods in which we live, the schools we attend, the health service we enjoy, the language we speak, the culture in which we grow, the political context in which we relate with one another. Changes in any one of the levels – or ecosystems – affects what goes on in all other levels.

As with all systems thinking, Bronfrenbrenner's approach encourages social workers to think and practice on a broad canvass. It has been most keenly adopted by child and family social workers. They realized that children affect and are affected by their parents, family, friends and school.

In turn their parents and the quality of their parenting are affected by their own history, development, relationships, marriage, support, income, housing, education, peers, school, social policy and culture. The ecosystems approach invites social workers and service users to think beyond the immediate and obvious. Why not develop closer working relationships with teachers and schools? Why not lobby local counsellors to support better nursery provision? Why not be part of a local health team?

The life model

One of the most comprehensive and well worked out ecological approaches to social work is that of Germain and Gitterman's *life model* (1996). They observe that individually we each struggle to stay in balance with our environment, that we need a *fit* between ourselves and the wider world in which we live. If the balance gets out of kilter, if the fit is no longer smooth, we experience *stress*. We feel we can't *cope*. That's when we experience personal difficulty. We might even become a social problem as we struggle with the strain between our personal needs, social constraints and economic limits. A disabled woman who can't get a job, never mind negotiate a thoughtless world of steps, revolving doors and head-height vending machines, is highly likely to feel stressed and angry, and with some justification.

Life modellers therefore aim to improve the fit between people and their environments. By working with individuals and families, groups and social networks, communities and political bodies, they try to reconfigure the ecological matrix in order to reduce stress and strain.

Reminders of employment rights, improvements to the physical environment, and maybe a bit of support and counselling might just do the trick for the disabled woman.

Not wholly successful

As Payne clarifies, systems and ecological approaches do provide a way of backing both individual change and social reform. Systems theory includes:

> ... work with individuals, groups and communities, and does not emphasise any particular method of intervention. Instead, it provides an overall way of describing things at any level, so that we can understand all interventions as affecting systems ... Workers choose theories appropriate to levels of intervention with which they are involved. They thus avoid sterile debates about whether

they are concerned with individual change or social reform. (Payne 2005a: 157)

As attractive and fun as ecological, systems and complexity theory are to the lay reader, there is no avoiding the fact that their origins are in biology, engineering, physics and mathematics. Ideas generated in the natural and mathematical sciences don't always translate well into the social sciences. They certainly stretch claims of relevance when adopted by applied social scientists including social workers. Perhaps this explains why the early promise of systems theory to create a grand practice theory has never fully been realized.

Root causes

Systemic thinking and ecological models encourage us to head upwards and outwards. However, in contrast, there has also been a steady tradition in social work that has valued digging down and deeper. Social reformers and radical practitioners insists we burrow below to peer beneath the political surface and examine the real root causes of service users' problems.

The word radical, of course, derives from the Latin, radix, for root. When the word radical is applied to an action or idea it implies an attempt to get to the root or origin of the matter. Radical social work therefore represents an attempt to examine the deep cause of things. Its practitioners demand fundamental changes in the political landscape and the economic base that supports social life. They make loud calls for social equality. It is time to hear what they have to say.

15
Radical Social Work

Religion and reform

Social work's movers and shakers, those who embrace causes, are motivated by a variety of reasons. Many early pioneers simply felt compassion and concern for the downtrodden, deprived and under-privileged. In many cases this was born of their religious faith. They adopted a practical approach to solving social problems. They got stuck in. Theory as such did not feature in their work.

The Unitarians were great advocates of social change. Quakers, too, have always held a strong sense of social responsibility that inevitably brought them into contact with the growing problems of poverty, moral decline and despair. For example:

'The Retreat' in York, a Quaker run innovation, provided warm, kind and decent care as well as treatment for the mentally ill. Peter Bedford helped set up a 'Soup Society' that provided food and home support for the poor families of London's East End. He also worked with juvenile offenders 'to bring them back to a decent way of life. (quoted in Young and Ashton 1956: 39).

Elizabeth Fry, as we heard earlier, was also a Quaker. It was her faith as much as her character that motivated her to be of social service and meet human need.

Others mixed religious principles with the early socialist move-ment. For example, the Christian Socialists, who influenced Octavia Hill, felt that there should be more 'brotherhood', co-operation and harmony between the middle and working classes. They supported education and the trade union movement.

Social surveys and the rise of sociology

Paralleling these early social work developments was the emergence of the new discipline of sociology with its concerns about the social order, inequality and what they might mean for social stability and change.

Sociology was also associated with what we now know as social surveys – attempts to map, calculate and quantify who were the poor, how many of them were there, where did they live, what was their income, and what were the conditions in which they lived. The results of these early statistical surveys often provided shocking evidence of what it was like to be poor.

One early example of the social survey was the classic study of poverty by Charles Booth, *The Life and Labour of the People in London*, carried out between 1889 and 1903. A similar survey was conducted by Seebohm Rowntree in the city of York. *Poverty: A Study of Town Life* was published in 1901.

In an attempt to be 'scientific' rather than simply be morally outraged, these sociological investigations were intent on finding out the 'facts'. The more solid the facts about social problems, the more it was felt that politicians would have to listen. Social change would therefore be brought about by rational, scientific enquiry. The facts would speak for themselves. Sociology at this time tended to be problem-focussed, and less analytical, less theoretical.

Such findings certainly influenced many key social reformers and political figures of the time. By the end of the nineteenth century more and more politicians began to realize that the poor were not responsible for their own desperate conditions. For example, Beatrice Webb, never one to mince her words, recalled her horror when she first saw 'the slums of great cities, the stagnant pools of deteriorated men and women . . . demoralizing their children and all new-comers, and perpetually dragging down each other into ever lower depths of mendacity, sickness and vice' (quoted in Woodroofe 1962: 50).

Webb originally worked for the Charity Organization Society which sought to help the poor based on Christian principles. However, she soon felt that charity wasn't the answer to meeting the needs of those who were worst off. She began to argue that it was inadequate housing, a lack of education and poor public health provision that caused poverty and deprivation. Some time later, Webb worked for Charles Booth on his London survey of the poor. Her general reading was wide and she became impressed with the sociological writings of Spencer and Compte.

Combining her first hand knowledge of poverty with the theoretical ideas of these early sociologists, she concluded that 'self-sacrifice for the good of the community was the greatest of all human characteristics.' (Spartacus 2008: 1).

In 1905, she was invited to serve as a member of the Royal Commission that was set up to look at the Poor Law. However, she disagreed with the more conservative majority report and, along with her husband Sidney Webb, she submitted a more radical minority report arguing for the end of the Poor Law. The way forward, she believed, was the universal provision of good quality health care and sound education. However, the Liberal government of the day rejected the Webbs' minority report and went with the findings of the majority.

Nevertheless, we see in the work of the Webbs the increasing use of social science theory and research to bring about social reform and change. Being poor was not part of the natural order. It was not the result of individual flaws and failings. It was largely 'man-made'. The answers therefore lay in collective action, via state provision, to improve the conditions of the vast numbers of poor that industrial societies threw up in their wake. And so it was that slowly, between the years 1906 and 1912, we began to see the first foundations of the welfare state being laid.

The energy of the Webbs and their associates was extraordinary. They joined the Fabian Society, helped found the London School of Economics in 1895, were very much involved with the beginnings of the Labour Party, and in 1913, along with friends, published a new political weekly magazine, *The New Statesman*. All three institutions continue to influence social and political thought even to this day.

Full Marx for social work

If sociological theory evolved to theorize the problems of modernity (the social fall-out of industrialization, urbanization, huge growths in population, and wide scale poverty and misery), it was social reformers rather than social workers who for much of the twentieth century were being influenced by social and political theory.

In the main, early social work stuck with its nineteenth century casework tradition, that is social work as function and not cause. Social work throughout this period was more responsive to what psychologists and humanists had to say. It was not really until the 1960s that social work recovered its interest in critical sociology and political theory. Whether coincidence or not, this was a time when many sociologists were reviving and re-working the writings of Karl Marx.

By the 1960s, more attention was beginning to be paid to the social consequences of capitalism. Capitalists create their wealth by owning the means of production. They exploit the physical and intellectual labour of their fellow men and women to produce goods and services. Although those who work – the working classes – do get paid, only a portion of the value of their labour is rewarded. The surplus value is retained, or in Marxist terms 'appropriated' by the owners of capital. In this way they get rich.

Through their control of the media, the political machinery, the law, and education, the rich and powerful also define the political and ideological climate in which the rest of us learn to think and act. Most of us tend to buy into the capitalist line that hard work, scarce talent and personal effort lead to success. The talented and hard-working deserve to be rewarded with wealth, and with wealth comes power.

It therefore follows that if you are poor or unsuccessful, you have failed and you only have yourself to blame. Those who put the individual before the group believe that inequality is inevitable in any society. In fact, it is by rewarding the hard-working and talented that societies grow and prosper.

To the extent the rich and powerful subtly, and sometimes not so subtly control the social and political agenda, the rest of us rarely question the order of things and the rightness of that order. We remain relatively powerless. In this analysis, the most disadvantaged people in society are those who have no 'labour' to sell.

If social value is measured by how much you produce, those who are no longer members, or never have been members of the labour force are without value. To be worthless is to be socially stigmatized. Deprived of key resources and suffering economic disadvantage, their lives are often stressful. Stress increases the risk of mental and physical health problems. Disadvantaged, disturbed or disaffected members of these groups are easily cast as a 'social problem' about which something should be done. These are the people whose behaviour should be contained, controlled, treated, subdued or punished.

Many social work clients are not wage earners. Even worse, from the point of view of capitalist economies, the majority of service users not only fail to produce wealth, they actually consume resources.

Social work service users include physically disabled people, people who are unable to work because of mental illness, old people (defined as 'spent labour'), lone parents, and learning disabled men and women. They can also include the unruly and unpredictable, the delinquent and criminal. The only exception recognized by capitalism is the potential of children. Children are valued because they represent 'future labour'. Child care and educational provisions therefore generally command larger slices of the national budget per capita than vulnerable adults or the dependent elderly.

Care and control

A Marxist analysis of capitalist economies defines two major service user groups. There are those who are classified as dependent and a drain on society's resources, provocatively defined as 'social junk' by Spitzer (1975). And there are those who are dangerous and disruptive, referred to as 'social dynamite' (Spitzer 1975). People who are dependent need to be maintained at a basic level of subsistence. They need *care*. Those who are disruptive, threatening, criminal and anti-social have to be *controlled*, or even locked away.

The functions of *care* and *control*, both carried out by social workers, are not always easy to reconcile in practice. They represent yet another strain in the character of social work and what the profession is asked to do by society. And just to hammer home the distinctions between care and control, governments spend more per capita on the disruptive, difficult and criminal who need to be controlled than they do on the dependent, vulnerable and depressed who need care.

Little surprise therefore that these sociological critiques of the iniquities of capitalism and the part it plays in the creation of human need and misery had great appeal to many social workers (for example, Corrigan and Leonard 1978, Jones 1983). Sociologically informed social workers felt it was not only folly to offer casework and therapy to 'clients', it was also immoral. The problems of the clients of social workers were not of their own making. They were the victims of an economic and political system that necessarily created massive inequalities, winners and losers, rich and poor.

The only moral position that can be adopted by social workers is to challenge the economic and political order that gives rise to so much disadvantage and misery. By taking a critical look at the social and personal effects of capitalism and the economic structures it sponsors, practitioners of this persuasion became known as Marxist or radical social workers, workers who radically questioned existing structures.

A radical analysis

The radical social worker needs to understand how the poor get to be poor. Only then will she recognize that the problems of old people, families in poverty, and those who have a mental illness are not problems of their own making but rather problems created by inequalities of money, power and authority.

Incidentally, the 1960s saw a big expansion in the number of universities. Sociology degrees, offered by many of the new universities, were also growing in popularity. One of the preferred occupational destinations of many of these newly minted sociology graduates was to pursue a career in social work. But armed with a sophisticated understanding of the nature of power and its impact on social structures, they began to question not only what social workers did but the way they did it. The social theories picked up from the universities began to drive radical social work practices.

One of the first targets of the radical critique was traditional casework practice. Underpinned by psychodynamic theory, casework was seen to be nothing more than a prop supporting capitalism and the economic order of an unequal and unfair society.

Under capitalism, the task of the traditional social worker is to control the behaviour of the dangerous and disturbed, cure the dysfunctional, and care for and contain the needy, the vulnerable, the socially inadequate, and the behaviourally incompetent.

Acting on behalf of society, social workers help mop up capitalism's casualties. They help manage and contain discontent. They paper over the cracks of a morally suspect economic system. In short, social workers are agents of social control, and the welfare state is the price that capitalism is prepared to pay for economic, social and political stability. By their actions, social workers, whether they realize it or not, support economic inequality and the vested interests of the privileged and powerful.

Casework was therefore seen as a confidence trick that duped the poor and oppressed them into accepting their station in life. The idea that casework was a 'con' inspired a sociologically literate workforce, radical practices, and a new magazine called, appropriately enough, *Case Con* launched in the early 1970s.

A radical agenda

Society is characterized by different groups struggling to wrest power, control and resources for their own benefit. The social order that the ruling classes seek to preserve, of course, is one that sustains their interests and wellbeing. Conflict between classes is therefore inevitable.

It is right and proper that those without power, authority and resources, whose needs are scarcely being met, should be helped to gain more power, more authority, and have their basic needs provided for. In challenging society to recognize the true causes of human need and misery, social workers will find themselves in conflict with those whose vested interests are being threatened.

Nevertheless, social workers should actively promote conflict between the haves and the have-nots. Increasing tension between the powerful and weak will eventually result in structural changes in the social and economic order. Only socialist and collectivist action will bring about social justice and equality. Inequality and injustice are simply the product of capitalist, liberal economics and what happens when society is based on letting people pursue their own interests unfettered by social restraint.

Acting on behalf of clients, radical social workers must struggle politically against the powers-that-be. The proper response to poverty and need is outrage – not care, not comfort, not containment. Rather, 'public issues' should be made out of 'private sorrows'. The aim is to push for a fairer distribution of society's resources, to change the social order. The true radical wants to change the political system to meet the needs of people and not change people to fit the political system.

Structural change

Mullaly (2003), Davis (2007) and others call their version of this approach *structural social work*. Structuralism is a reaction against humanism that sees the individual as a self-directing, creative force (Seidman 2004: 162). Structuralism looks to forces beyond the individual to explain social life. It is clear that personal problems are caused by social, economic and political structures and interests. These structures shape people's lives and experience.

There is no getting away from the fact that the majority of service users live in relative states of poverty and deprivation. It is this fact that needs to be addressed, not the behavioural and psychological consequences of living in conditions of stress.

It is society's social structures therefore that have to change if people are to be free of domination. Within this perspective, the quality of people's personal and social experience should take precedence over economic goals.

Social welfare in general and social work in particular are well placed to help bring about these qualitative changes in which people can experience equality of treatment and a sense of belonging. Learning disabled adults should enjoy a decent wage for the work they do. Old people should campaign to have higher pensions and warmer houses. And if stress is caused by not feeling in control, then giving disabled people, old people, people with learning disabilities and single parents more control will reduce stress, and increase mental health and wellbeing. Or as Mick McGahey, a lifelong communist put it in 1986 as he approached his own retirement, 'I will join the pensioners and create hell among the pensioners!'

From radical to critical

The radical social work answer therefore is collective action. The aim is to work towards a society based on equality, justice and involvement. However, although the radical agenda has had some success, it has never fully realized its early ambitions.

On further analysis, a more subtle form of sociological reasoning was called for. This became known as critical social theory and it has helped sponsor some extremely interesting developments in social work theory and practice.

16

Critical Social Work

Critical social theory

Although there is a great deal of intellectual excitement around the idea of being a radical social worker, it is quite hard to translate all this political fervour into some kind of day-to-day practice. It was all very well for the sociologists and political theorists to expose the true nature of liberal, capitalist economic democracies and how their systems, including state welfare services supported the interests of the rich and powerful, but all this social theorizing left social work sympathizers feeling either guilty or helpless. Moreover, there were early signs that Marxist sociology, on which so much of the original ideas of radical social work were based, was beginning to go out of fashion.

The sociological sciences themselves were moving on. New thinkers were taking our understanding of power and ideology in new directions. Fresh ways of explaining how social structures affected personal psychology were being mapped out. By the 1980s, there were the first glimpses of how some of these ideas might influence and inform social work practice. A handful of researchers and theorists continued to follow developments in the social sciences and feed them into the social work psyche. But this time the ideas seemed to have practical possibilities.

As part of this transition a number of social work academics were busy trying to find theoretical and practical ways forward. They accepted that social workers were acting as agents of social control, but felt that by helping working class clients to understand how their problems were being created by the unfair workings of a system that favoured the rich and powerful, social workers were also raising people's political awareness (Corrigan and Leonard 1978). The more clients understood the true nature of their situation, the more they could recover some power and control from the state.

More powerful still, group action could lead to demands for improved housing or having a greater voice in community developments. By banding together, the users of services could argue for changes in policy and legislation. Clients who had a mental illness might challenge aspects of the legislation that was denying them some of their basic rights and freedoms. Women who had lost a child by adoption might question whether it was fair to write them out of the story once their child had been placed in a new family.

It was out of these mood changes in sociology and political theory, and the growing frustrations felt with radical social work that more practical applications of sociology began to be fashioned. By the 1990s these newer 'radical' practices and the theories supporting them began to be referred to as *critical social work*.

Critical theory and social work

Critical social work was inspired by many of the ideas being generated by critical social theory. Critical theorists examine the socially constructed character of society. They show how ruling and powerful social groups are able to justify injustice and inequality by their control of the language, media, education, political agenda and terms of debate.

For example, Habermas (1968) thinks that knowledge is structured by social interests. However, he also thought that we all wish to be free of unnecessary constraint, that we want to be *free from* unreasonable limits, and *free to* explore and express our own individuality. We should all be free to contribute to the social discourse in which we are all embedded and have our being. For Habermas, the 'values of democracy, justice, equality, and autonomy are not arbitrary or irrational but are the very preconditions of communication, the hidden telos towards which everyday life is directed' (Seidman 2004: 126).

Critical social workers continued to argue that the traditional influences of cognitive, behavioural and psychodynamic psychologies were not only irrelevant but also part of the problem. These psychologies helped social workers blame or pathologize clients. It meant that social workers took their eyes off the real cause of people's difficulties, namely unjust social structures and unequal distributions of power and resources.

However, many felt that a Marxist analysis of power and domination in crude class and economic terms was too simplistic. It didn't seem to explain the oppression and domination suffered by many other groups in society. Women were being oppressed by men, children by adults, minority ethnic groups by majority ethnic groups, and gay men and lesbian women by heterosexual men and women.

Marxism applied to the workplace. It spoke of class. But issues of power and domination seemed to saturate ordinary everyday life as well. This called for a new analysis, one that was *critical* of society, of the politics of everyday life and routine relationships.

Nevertheless, it was still recognized that the big features of the way societies were ordered and structured reflected the interests of the powerful. Furthermore, by controlling such things as the media, technology, politics, education and the terms in which social issues were conceived and conducted, the control of the powerful actually reached down to the level of everyday life and relationships.

For example, the law sets the terms in which child abuse is perceived and handled. The media is particularly influential in affecting the way we think about people and events. It affects the way those in employment view those unable to work. It colours the way women are portrayed and how men might relate to them. It sways how majority ethnic groups might perceive minority ethnic groups.

The postmodern turn

A series of groundbreaking books by the French sociologist, Michel Foucault, appeared to reverse much of the direction of conventional Marxist theory. Rather than look at power as something that was exercised over the rest of us by rich capitalists who owned the means of production and controlled the state apparatus, Foucault explored how power operated in everyday relationships between men and women, black people and white people, disabled people and able-bodied people.

Foucault (1969, 1977, 1980) argued that social theory must abandon its attempts to try and explain and encompass all aspects of social life as Karl Marx and Max Weber and other classical social theorists had tried to do. All that social thinkers can do is to try and understand relationships, values, power and politics at a local, provisional level. Moreover, power shifts and evolves. It doesn't stand still.

In Foucault's world, there are no deep, unifying patterns of meaning. There are no grand theories so beloved by Modernity. There is no utopia, no social progress or golden road to the best of all possible worlds. Unlike classical sociology, born of the Enlightenment, there

Power, in this sense, therefore becomes more insidious, less obvious, less overt. Anyone who steps outside these 'normalities' is pathologized; they are deemed mad or deviant, abnormal or ill, dangerous or deluded.

> Governmentality is a more active form of power than institutionalised control because it concentrates on regulating individuals from the 'inside'. Power is de-centred, with individuals playing an active role in their own self-governance. (Webb 2006: 15).

But we might ask, in what way does being disabled, gay, female, or old actually define the self? An individual might be old or black or gay, but this does not and should not define them and who they are.

Once defined by dominant discourses (say, those of medicine, social work, welfare legislation, politicians, or the media), people are easier to isolate, treat and control. In their efforts, the state and dominant discourses then aim to 'normalize' deviant subjects. Doctors 'treat' the insane. Social workers 'police' dysfunctional families. Probation officers monitor and control offenders.

To the extent that social workers think and practice within the language of dominant discourses, their knowledge and power contributes to the domination experienced by disabled people, those who have a mental illness, and families who upset the sensibilities of the middle classes.

Foucault was interested in how particular groups developed ways of thinking about, talking about and defining their bit of the world. This also meant that all those who fell into that group's area of interest became caught up in the group's 'discourse', their way of seeing things. Those without expertise and power found themselves being defined, explained and dealt with in terms of the dominant groups' language and interests.

Foucault looked at the power of doctors to define illness, psychiatrists to speak with authority about mental illness, and sociologists and psychologists to explain criminality and how it should be treated. Specialists, whether they happen to be doctors or educationalists, social workers or criminologists lay claim to the 'truth' about which only they could speak, pronounce and adjudicate. As Illich famously describes them, doctors, teachers and social workers are really the 'dis-abling professions'. Their 'expert' solutions perpetuate the oppressed conditions of service users.

Those about whom the experts speak lack the power to challenge the terms of the dominant group's discourse. They are oppressed by the expert's or dominant group's definitions, explanations and treatments. As Marx and Engel's observed, the ideas of the ruling class are the ruling ideas, the ones in which we all find ourselves psycho-logic-ally embedded (Marx and Engels 1965: 60). Those who control the 'discourse' have the power. The discourse serves their interests and not those who are caught up in its language.

Language, particularly the language of professionals, is never neutral. It conveys meaning. It defines the service user's experience. It constructs the sense of self and how it is to be understood. 'Language is therefore about much more than words – it is about *power*' (Fook 2007: 66 emphasis original).

Critical and reflective social work practices

This analysis of 'the politics of every day life' gave social workers a much more workable opportunity to apply social theory to the world they knew, the world of everyday relationships. Issues such as domestic violence or racial discrimination could be articulated with greater power and clarity.

In this analysis, there is no big, over-riding 'grand' theory that tries to explain everything. Rather, the way power and domination are played out in day-to-day relationships allowing some groups to maintain control while others suffer oppression, is where the analysis must focus. This is exactly the level at which social workers operate. Although domination is achieved through the way society structures relationships between the powerful and the oppressed, oppression itself is experienced personally. Critical social theory began to influence social work as it sponsored a range of value-based practices.

To help social workers recognize the insidious part that inequalities of power play in the problems experienced by service users, they are encouraged to develop practices that are critically reflective.

The *critically reflective practitioner* is one who adopts a critical perspective on what she knows and values. She recognizes the key role that power plays in shaping both what the service user experiences and what the social worker does (Thompson and Thompson 2008a). The critically reflective practitioner tries to remain aware of the part that power plays at the personal and professional level. Social workers who remain unaware and insensitive to the significance of power run the risk of unwittingly reinforcing existing inequalities and oppressive practices (Thompson and Thompson 2008b).

Word power

Language is the currency of discourse and so great attention is paid to language and how it is used. How do dominant groups talk about those who are relatively powerless? If we alter our language, can we alter the way people perceive and relate to one another? Can the words used change the balance of power in relationships?

We can see the influence of critical theory and postmodernism on strengths-based, solution-focused and constructive social work. They all share an interest in language, meaning and power. We must be aware of how words shape our experience. We must be alert to the power of words, who is using them and what effects their use has on others.

It was awareness of these subtle 'micro-politics' of everyday life that lead to shifts in much of social work's terminology. We saw in Chapters 12 and 13 that to talk about the 'mentally ill' implies that it is the mental illness that defines a person's essential being. This was seen as diminishing. Rather, being mentally ill is not a definition of who a person is. Some people simply have a mental illness just as they might have influenza.

Language that demeans other people is an attempt to reduce their worth. It tries to deny them power or the right to protest. Paying attention to how we refer to people is therefore a small but important step in creating relationships in which people value, respect and appreciate one another.

Similarly, no longer were service users described as the 'mentally handicapped' but rather they were people with learning difficulties. The offensive use of many words to describe women, black or old people was attacked as sexist, racist or ageist. Such descriptions are literally the language of oppression. Even the term client was subject to scrutiny with many preferring to think about people as 'service users' although there is always the nagging anxiety that social work's policing of some its vocabulary makes it an easy target for accusations of political correctness.

However, we might note in passing that not everyone is happy with the term 'service user'. Some cognitive-behavioural social workers don't like the term and prefer to stick with the word client (Sheldon and Macdonald 2009). Some surveys show that the majority of 'service users' of psychiatric services still prefer to be described as patients (mentioned in Dalrymple 2008). The observant reader will have noticed that I have used all three terms – client, patient, service user – throughout these pages, not indiscriminately, but mainly to reflect either the historical context, the theoretical outlook under consideration, or the professional discipline being discussed.

Critical social work helps service users analyze their situation in terms of who holds the power. Who has labelled them? What does the label mean and suggest? Who is telling people what they need and what is best for them? What is the effect of these labels on those who get labelled? How much freedom and control over their own needs and circumstances do users actually have?

If you have a visual impairment, wouldn't you know best how your needs should be met? You would be open to advice. You would certainly want to know what the latest technological developments were that might improve the quality of your life. But when the resources are designed, delivered and deployed, you would expect your voice to be the loudest. You'd expect people to listen and hear how you think your needs might best be met.

Becoming aware

One of the key ideas to emerge out of these developments was the concept of *conscientization*. Simply defined, this meant helping those who suffer oppression realize not only that they are being oppressed, but how this oppression is being achieved. The cause of their problems is not the result of personal failings or flaws, rather it is the consequence of political injustice and an unequal distribution of power, resources and opportunities.

Many oppressed groups believe that their failures and problems are of their own making. They haven't tried hard enough. They are personally flawed, inadequate, incompetent. Under a critical analysis, many service users have a 'false consciousness' of the true origins of their problems and difficulties. The way societies are ordered is not pre-ordained. If they could become aware of how their subjugation and experience of inequality comes about, not only is this insight empowering it can also inspire people to do something about it.

The women's movement referred to a similar idea as *consciousness-raising*. Social orders, structures and relationships can be changed if people become aware and join together, become conscious and act collectively. Passive acceptance of the way things are is a recipe for continued oppression.

So resist other people's definitions of who you are, whether these definitions are delivered by welfare professionals, psychological experts or state legislation. Claim your own identity. Believing that we are agents of our destiny not only energizes us, it will lead to change (Fook 2002). Talk with fellow travellers. Act together. As ever, there is always strength in numbers. We experience support when others share and know our experience. Take control and fight for change. This is the critical social work agenda.

This mission to raise self-awareness and the consciousness of those subject to oppression and domination demands a particular kind of social work practice. The appeal is not to scientific-based evidence. The philosophy is one that believes that we create change, including changing our selves and our behaviour, as we talk with other people. We're back to the importance of the language used between social worker and service user. The conversation, the dialogue should be reflective and critical in tone. Collaboration between social workers and service users is key. Discussion and analysis lead to awareness, and awareness encourages action.

The divided self

Many people experience a tension between how they are defined and treated by the objective world of cultural expectations, social laws, and economic status and the subjective world of their own experience. When these two worlds of the self – the self seen as 'object' and the self experienced as 'subject' – become significantly out-of-line people feel alienated. The sense of who one actually is and who one could potentially be never connect. Feminists were among the first to explore these ideas. They were acutely aware that women relate to men in what is in many respects a 'man's world', a world defined and controlled by men for men.

As part of the move towards a critical social work practice, the women's movement and feminist theory, along with anti-racist and anti-discriminatory practices proved to be important trailblazers.

17

Feminist Social Work

Feminism

Pioneers of what eventually became known as critical social work were often foreshadowed by the women's movement and then by more theoretically savvy feminists. Feminist social workers took early advantage of the slogan 'the personal is the political'. The injustices and inequalities suffered by women are not the result of personal troubles, rather, they are social and political in origin.

Feminist practitioners also noted that not only were most clients women, but most social workers were female. These facts alone ought to make a feminist perspective the bedrock of sound practice (Hanmer and Statham 1999).

Women needed to understand that the way they perceived and experienced themselves was actually being defined and determined by men. The use of language, the stereotypes held, the expectations made all too often placed women in a one-down position.

Ideologically, women live in a man-made world, one that suits male interests. In this world, women are expected to accept that they will be judged in terms of their competence as lovers and mothers, wives and carers, sexual objects and paragons of virtue. These 'measures' saturate the content of magazines, newspapers, music, soap operas and male 'humour'.

Feminist theories applied these powerful insights to try and make sense of women's experience, including their oppressed position in society (Orme 2009). One of the major aims was to help women understand how social structures affected social relationships and how both of these subtly shaped their experience and thinking, assumptions and expectations.

By becoming aware (self-conscious) about how experience is shaped by social and economic structures, language and relationships, the hope is that women can free themselves of oppression, particularly oppression by men defined as patriarchy. Only then can they reclaim control of who they are and how they are.

The personal really is the political. So many social, economic, occupational and moral arrangements suit the interests of men. Within these arrangements and the assumptions that support them, women are devalued and disempowered. All such arrangements and assumptions have to be challenged.

Intimately bound with these matters are issues of reproduction and care – care of children, care of dependent relatives. Care is rarely paid for. It is not highly valued in terms of esteem and status. And yet care is fundamental to the successful conduct of family life, social support and the smooth running of society.

Feminists quite rightly note that it is women who provide the vast bulk of personal, family and community care. Even the assumption that women are by nature and by role best suited to be carers can be questioned, no matter what value is placed on care.

Liberal and radical feminism

Liberal feminists aim to reduce inequality and champion the right of both sexes to have equal opportunities at school, and in the family, workplace and the economic arena.

Feminist practices are egalitarian. They value partnership with and participation by service users. Some of the key principles of feminist practice identified by Dominelli (2002) include: value women's strength and recognize their diversity; support women as they seek to control and determine the content of their own lives; understand that social structures define personal experience; seek collective solutions to personal problems; and be prepared to work with men.

Whereas liberal feminists argue that there should be no relevant differences between the sexes, radical feminists recognize that there are differences between the sexes across a range of physical and psychological attributes but they go on to argue that these differences should receive equal value (Dominelli 2002, Orme 2009).

The differences should be celebrated and not used to degrade, depress and disadvantage women. The differences should also lead to the acceptance of different ways of doing things between the sexes. The use of formal rules and task analysis might appeal to men as they try to reach a decision. Women might find open discussion and collaborative relationships more conducive to good outcomes. This distinction might have important implications for the practice and management of social work cases and welfare agencies, the way power and authority are defined and exercised, and the way promotions and career opportunities are played out.

Collective solutions

Consciousness-raising can take place between worker and service user as together they analyse and reflect on the state of a relationship or the way a woman has been blinkered into limiting her own horizons and ambitions. Consciousness-raising tends to be most effective when people who share the same oppression come together. Being with fellow subjects speeds up awareness. Insights can be gained as people share experiences. Group support gives women strength and encourages self-belief. Collective action to change a policy or fight for a resource also becomes possible.

This is a reminder that so often different social work theories reach similar practice conclusions. In this case, social skills training, strengths perspectives, radical social work, feminist practices, and as we shall see in the next chapter, anti-oppressive and empowerment approaches all value bringing people together, whether in groups or community organizations, who share a similar need, experience or problem.

It is the case that being with others in the same position offers the opportunity to act together to bring about change. It might become clear to a group of female mental health service users that social isolation is a major risk factor triggering their anxiety and depression. So why not continue meeting as a group? Why not provide each other with support and friendship? Why not tell and share stories then write a new script? Why not try saying no to medically prescribed anti-depressants? Maybe this is the way to raise self-esteem, confidence and wellbeing. Some of these challenges were creatively met in the following example.

Emily was a mental health social worker attached to a medical General Practice. The practice had an inner-city location. There was a lot of poverty, social need and deprivation. The doctors in the practice grew concerned about the number of female patients they were seeing who came in feeling tired, under stress and depressed. The idea of just giving them anti-depressants seemed too easy and anyway, they felt, it was probably avoiding the real issue of what was causing their despair. They asked the social worker to think about the problem.

An analysis of the patients' case notes allowed Emily to identify a number of common factors. The women were all married or in a heterosexual relationship. The majority had school-age children. Most had been making appointments to see a doctor off and on for a number of years complaining of things such as tiredness, feeling run down, anxiety, stress, and a lack of energy and purpose. A sense of helplessness and hopelessness seemed to seep through each page of the medical notes.

Emily identified eight women who had made the most number of appointments over the past 3 years. She met each of them individually and invited them along to meet the other seven women, explaining that she felt they had much in common and that perhaps it would be helpful to look at matters together.

The mood of the first sessions reflected the flat state of the women but Emily persevered. However, the eight women kept returning, some saying that at least it got them out of the house. Gradually, though, the women began to share their experiences. Most had not had particularly happy childhoods. They felt that marriage or children might be the way to find contentment but they only seemed to bring more misery and distress. Their partners were invariably unsupportive. Some men were needy and a few were violent. Although the children were loved, the mothers felt they had no energy to be the kind of mothers they really wanted to be.

Nevertheless, as Emily had hoped, the weekly discussions in which stories were shared began to have an affect. Mutual support was offered. Feelings of being alone and isolated lessened. The mood lightened, ever so slightly. However, what set the group off in an entirely new, but ultimately positive direction was a session in which Emily described some research on depressed women she had come across by George Brown as his colleagues which she thought might be of interest (Brown and Harris 1978, Brown et al 1995).

The research findings that most captured the group's interest were to do with the relationship histories of women who were are greatest risk of depression. Many of the research subjects had childhoods in which there had been loss of a mother through death, divorce or abandonment followed by rather uncaring, low empathy parenting by their fathers or their new partners.

However, what the group identified with most was the finding that many of the research subjects described by Brown and his colleagues felt trapped in marriages and relationships that were undermining and lowering of self-esteem. They experienced humiliation as partners had affairs, constantly put them down, or squandered money on drugs, alcohol and gambling. There seemed no escape from these needy, 'useless' and insecure men.

The two words that came out of the research that most excited the group were 'humiliation' and 'entrapment'. These words, they felt, described their lives. Women who had low self-esteem, and felt trapped and humiliated in relationships were most at risk of feeling helpless, hopeless and full of despair. They felt they lacked control over their own lives. Feeling in control, they learned from Emily, was one of the best predictors of a positive, high self-esteem, energetic approach to life. Feeling defeated and in a situation of no escape made people feel helpless and depressed. They learned that having a confidante was good for psychological health.

Having grasped these ideas and seeing how they related to their own lives, the women in the group began to plan and discuss how they could recover control over their own lives. They confided in each other. The women encouraged and supported each other in coming up with a plan to increase the amount of control they could enjoy in their own lives. Each plan was a personal one, but there was much sharing, support and suggestion. Two women felt strong enough to leave their partners. Another got a part-time job as a care assistant, something which she's always wanted to do, but had been mocked in her ambitions by her husband. Two other women not only got their young children into the same play-group, they both became helpers.

A year after the group had formally last met, Emily reviewed the intervention. Two women felt they had slipped back into the hopelessness of their marriages. Three, including the two who had left their husbands, had become good friends and reported that their lives had improved significantly. The remaining three, although not claiming they had turned their lives around, nevertheless described feeling better, less intimidated and less helpless. They said the group has helped them feel a little more confident. None of them had taken anti-depressants for at least six months.

The personal is the political

Radical social change therefore comes about not by overthrowing the ruling classes but by changing people's subjective understanding and experience. Once consciousness has been raised, the behaviour and actions of individuals and groups will change. Power will begin to flow towards the previously powerless.

In this analysis, it becomes clear that women must recover control of their own experience. There is a strong strand of personal growth, development and self-realization in feminist practices. Personal change can help women feel stronger and more empowered, and with power, feelings of freedom and choice will increase. A battered wife finally finds the strength to leave her violent husband. A group of young mothers agree to lobby the council for better child care facilities.

In so many areas of practice, feminist social workers have led the way. However, close on their heels, and adding their own unique analysis and insights, are practitioners who recognize that not only women, but many other groups are also suffering discrimination and oppression. From a social work point of view, these discriminations and oppressions are obviously things to be against and so arose a powerful tide of anti-discriminatory and anti-oppressive practices.

18

Anti-oppressive Practices and Empowerment

Anti-oppressive practices

Feminist social workers showed how the analysis of social structures could be linked to a sensitive understanding of an individual's personal experience. They paved the way for a range of critical social work practices.

The appearance of critical sociological theory also helped drive social work back to its interests in values, language and social justice. It was in the middle of these busy times that other related theories and practices began to take shape. Anti-racist social work made an early appearance soon followed by a number of anti-discriminatory, anti-oppressive and culturally sensitive approaches. These approaches shared much of the analytic force of feminist and critical social work theories.

It was recognized that many groups including disabled people, people with a mental illness, gay men and lesbian women, and older people as well as women and black people experienced discrimin-ation. Many individuals experienced discrimination on several fronts. For example, being black and female, or having both a physical and learning disability could make you feel doubly oppressed.

Valuing difference

Discrimination implies people being treated differently *and* unfairly on grounds that have no justifiable moral relevance. Skin colour or gender or age are not relevant differences when it comes to treating people unequally in terms of respect and rights, resources and opportunities.

Furthermore, difference should not be 'pathologized'. The other person's culture and traditions should not be seen as a weakness or deficit (Payne 2005a: 275). For example, a dominant culture might view another culture's parenting practices in a negative light, or view certain behaviours as odd, disturbed and symptomatic of mental illness. If this is the case, we need to stop and think. We need to take careful stock before jumping to conclusions.

Anti-discriminatory practice sought to bring together the many ideas about difference and oppression into a single theory. And once again, we find that critical social theory and its analysis of inequality and injustice, power and domination, social structure and discourse was providing the intellectual energy that was driving the new practices.

For example, racism was clearly a reality for many black people living in a predominantly white society. However, what anti-racist and anti-discriminatory practices brought to the analysis was an appreciation of both structural and *cultural* factors. There were certainly issues of social injustice and inequality. But there were also matters of identity, culture, religion and prejudice to consider.

There was broad agreement that different cultures should respect and *be sensitive to* each other's traditions, character, religion and practices. Indeed, multiculturalists – those who recognize and value the benefits of diversity and cultural difference – argued that societies were enriched when different cultures were able to live together. Each cultural group could be inspired by the family, artistic and social traditions that other communities brought to the social whole.

The social fabric would be held together and strengthened by the bonds of respect and recognition. Unity would be achieved by tolerating diversity. Social work practice should reflect these values. Practitioners should show a courteous interest and respect for the different ways in which people go about their lives, whether in matters of food, religious observance or dress.

Being in a position of some power themselves, social workers (and their agencies) must be mindful of their own potential for being oppressive and discriminatory. Social workers have the power to apply for the removal of children from their parents. Along with doctors, they can deprive people with a mental illness of their liberty and take them to a mental health hospital. Social workers have these powers, but they must exercise them with awareness, thought and sensitivity.

Professional discrimination can be explicit, perhaps seen in the way a white worker makes assumptions about a black person's needs. Social workers will bring their own histories, their own cultural make-up and their own biases into practice. It is therefore incumbent on all workers to be critical and self-reflective. Or discrimination can be implicit and institutional. The way a department words its policies, defines need or allocates resources could disadvantage certain service user groups or people from particular cultures.

It is by analyzing the meaning of their own experience that all oppressed groups recover control. Working in partnership and supporting oppressed people gain more power allows their voice to be heard (Dalrymple and Burke 1995). Collaborative and egalitarian practices identify the knowledge and skills that a group might need to develop if power is to increase and aims be achieved. Empowering people helps them improve resources. With a stronger voice, they can push for changes in policy and practice.

Re-valuing social work

In contrast to social work seen as scientific and evidence-based, what we see in radical and critical practices is a reminder that social work can also be about moral issues. There is therefore an explicit political agenda. If the radical analysis is right, the social worker's mission is to change the moral climate, not individual behaviour.

The increasing respect for service users and the drive to equalize power relationships inevitably lead to projects with clients that are collaborative in nature. Many of these partnerships aim to *transform* the institutions that deliver traditional client services so that the manner and content of what they do not only respects service users, it empowers them. And who knows, perhaps consultation with users might lead to more suitable services and tailor-made resources.

Perhaps the biggest contribution of radical and critical social work theories has been to recover social work's values and put them centre stage. For example, Healy (2005: 188) observes that for anti-oppressive practitioners, social justice should lie at the heart of all good social work.

What we see throughout the critical agenda is the challenge to social workers that they should be culturally aware. There needs to be a structural analysis of power – who has it, who hasn't, and why. Power also affects interpersonal dynamics, the way organizations behave, and how services are delivered. Practitioners should be ever-mindful of how inequality, whether based on class, gender, physical and intellectual ability, culture and ethnicity, limit and oppress certain groups, and then aim to do something about it.

Empowerment and advocacy

Running as a theme through much of radical, critical and anti-discriminatory practices is the idea of empowerment. It promotes a way of working with, and relating to service users based on equality, partnership and transparency. It gives service users a voice and recognizes their rights.

Power means that you can determine the content of your own experience. You have the ability to control the environment to suit your needs. You have a say in plans and decisions that affect you. You have a right to be heard.

Working with individuals and groups who suffer disadvantage, inequality or injustice first requires the practitioner to help people take stock of their situation (Lee 2001, Adams 2008). Out of these early discussions and recognition of shared needs and concerns, the group forms. It identifies problems, begins to analyze why they exist and who, or what, perpetuate them. Slowly, individuals and members of the group not only begin to make better sense of their situation, they begin to see ways of doing something about it. They begin to feel stronger, more empowered, and so less helpless, less passive. At this stage, they begin to see what courses of action can be taken to change their experience.

The following two examples are taken from Robert Adams' scene setting book on empowerment, participation and social work (Adams 2008: 112).

Survivors Speak Out was formed in 1986. The group included many patients who had been in mental health hospitals. Traditionally, the voice of mental health patients was rarely heard. Doctors, nurses, managers and politicians knew little of what it felt like to be a patient of the mental health services in general, and mental health hospitals in particular. By joining forces with sympathetic professionals, mental health patients not only learned to 'speak out' but in the process they also discovered they had the power to change practices and affect policy.

The Asian Resource Centre in Handsworth, Birmingham 'came about through a grassroots initiative by people involved in a multicultural centre called Action Centre. Workers involved at the time noted the need for a centre specifically designed to meet the needs of Asian people' (Adams 2008: 155). Local people were becoming aware that their needs were not being met by the formal and local statutory services and it was around this issue that the idea of a centre formed. Advice work at the centre quickly led to a wide range of projects including 'Asian Elders', 'Women's Welfare Rights', and the setting up of various pressures groups as well as providing practical help with issues of immigration, sexism and nationality.

At root, empowerment is about social justice (Rees 1991). It is about increasing equality and fairness through shared support and action. People recognize what issues are important to them and decide what should be done about them. Empowerment 'redirects the radical analysis towards work with individuals, groups and communities, rather than political or social action to combat social injustices . . .' (Payne 2005b).

Working together

Many social work principles support service user empowerment. Client self-determination, equality, and democratic relationships have to be present and practised if the promotion of empowerment is to be genuine. Yet again, we hear that self-help groups have a particularly good track-record. Working with others who share the same need or experience or suffer the same oppression is an effective way of helping people become aware of their situation. Groups are therefore empowering (Mullender and Ward 1991).

The more people become involved in determining their own destiny, the higher will be their self-esteem. They grow in confidence. And when group members learn that knowledge is power, they demand to know, to be kept informed, to be given information.

For example, over the past two or three decades, physically disabled people have had considerable success lobbying for social change. Wheelchair users have gained better access to and around buildings. They have made job discrimination on grounds of disability illegal. It is the attitudes of others and the architecture of building that disables people who get around in a wheelchair or who have a visual impairment, not being in a wheelchair or being visually impaired per se. Change the reactions of people or the physical lay-out of places, and the disabled individual suffers no loss of value or physical disadvantage. This analysis shows that disability is, in fact, a socially constructed experience (Campbell and Oliver 1996).

When a policy changes or a building has been adapted, the cause has been won. And both the success of the cause and the manner of its achievement are empowering. A bit more of your life comes under your control.

From social reform to critical practice

Over the last few chapters we have been following a development that had its origins in the mid-nineteenth century. Early reformers were people who pursued social causes. Sociology arose in part to provide empirical and theoretical ammunition to support the causes and the reforms they championed.

A century later, Marxism provided social workers with a particularly interesting and powerful theoretical framework in which to think about social work and service users. It gave rise to a variety of radical social work practices in which power and who has it were of central interest.

However, the appearance of new philosophical, political and sociological theories in the form of postmodernism re-oriented many radical practitioners towards a more critical perspective.

Critical social work retained its interest in power, but added new elements to its analysis and practice. These included recognizing the subtle but pervasive part that language plays in constructing our social reality. Moreover, language is in a constant state of flux. Its meanings are forever being contested by different groups and their interests. Established meanings are the result of powerful groups imposing their definitions of how we should define and therefore see things and people. This approach is referred to as *poststructuralism*.

'Poststructuralism is a kind of permanent rebellion against authority, that of science and philosophy but also the church and the state' (Seidman 2004: 168). As it 'de-constructs' words, language and meaning, poststructuralism celebrates difference and variety in social life. These ideas went down particularly well with a range of newly emerging approaches including feminist, anti-discriminatory and anti-oppressive practices.

As we have seen, common to many versions of radical and critical practices is a strong critique of most psychological, medical and pathological models of social work. However, some observers feel that being so fiercely critical of traditional psychosocial casework is in danger of ignoring important psychological components of our human-make up. Critical social work's strong critique of psychological thinking 'accompanied by the prioritization of structural analysis of clients' experiences, can lead social workers to neglect individual psychological and personal factors that may contribute substantially to elevated risk in some contexts, such as child protection, mental health and work in corrections' (Healy 2005: 189).

Not all clients experience social work interventions as oppressive. There is a great variety of client experience that the anti-discriminatory/oppressive approach fails to acknowledge, particularly when the emphasis is solely on structural factors (Healy 2005: 189). Social workers very often have to balance parents' needs with the needs of their children, or the needs of an elderly dependent mother and her over-tired, over-stressed caring daughter.

More general still, care, change, cure and control, those four uncomfortable bedfellows, have characterized social work since its inception. Embracing all four has never been easy. There have been cuckoo-like tendencies by both reforming social workers and casework practitioners to throw out of the social work nest one or other of cure, change, care or control. But there is an argument to be made that together these four elements actually comprise social work and perhaps what unites them is something more pervasive, more encompassing, that carries whatever social workers choose to do. This is the social work relationship.

19

Relationship-based Social Work

The two faces of social work

Social work arises in that space where individuals and society meet. Societies take an interest in what their citizens do and how they behave. In the case of social work, it is welfare laws and social policies that reflect the nature of that interest. From the perspective of individuals, they need to take note of what their society allows and prohibits, supports and values.

It is also the case that individuals need to be aware of what society and its systems can do for them. Society can protect and provide as well as monitor and control. Disturbed and disturbing people can be helped as well as managed.

Janus-like, social work has always had to look both ways. It finds itself representing the individual to society (this is what it is like to be poor and vulnerable), and representing society to the individual (what society expects and what it can do for you). Both *care* of the weak and *control* of the unruly have defined social work from the beginning. It therefore seems inevitable that compassion and correction, welfare and justice are bound to give social work something of a split identity.

Care encourages practices that empathize, support and protect. Its theoretical sympathies tend towards the humanities and religious traditions, particularly those that explore the part that love and compassion play in human relationships.

Control on the other hand seeks to restrict and contain the ugly side of human behaviour and personal experience. However, even better than controlling people is to *cure* them – of their bad ways or their unhappy experiences, then they don't even need to be controlled. The aim is to change people who are problems and help people who have problems. The theories that underpin social work as control and social work as cure are those of the applied social sciences.

Cure and treatment-based interventions have a strong preference for theories and practices that are scientific and evidence-based. These are the cognitive and behavioural, task-oriented and solutions-focused approaches that occupied us in earlier chapters.

Since its beginnings, then, social work has pursued a complex agenda, siding with the weak one moment, and admonishing the wayward the next. Unfortunately, working with the poor and representing the powerless and dangerous to the rich and powerful is not a comfortable place for any occupation to be. It's all too easy to end up pleasing no-one.

On the one hand there is the danger that service users see social workers as agents of state control. On the other, there is the risk that the state and the media dismiss social workers as naïve 'do-gooders' who side with the dangerous, degenerate and undeserving. This partly explains why both users and the public so often view social workers with ambivalence – whose side are they on?

The worker-user relationship

The relationship between the state and the individual is subject to constant change as the big ideas generated by political and social theorists alter the way we think about individuals and society. As we have seen, social work inevitably gets caught up in these big ideas as they sweep through history. We've already considered theories that argue that if the life of oppressed service users is to improve, then society has to change and social reform must be pursued.

We've also met theories that are quite happy to promote individual change, whether it's to cure problem behaviours or treat distressed minds.

However, what we have not yet considered is the medium in which all these different theories and their practices take place, namely the relationship between the social worker and service user. Does the relationship itself have any effect or value independent of the theories and practices it carries?

The importance of the personal relationship

Relationship-based social work has been part of social work's make-up since it first began to take shape in the nineteenth century. Here is

Elizabeth Fry, the great prison reformer, showing the value of the 'use of self' and self-disclosure. On a visit to women and children in London's Newgate Prison she was at once:

> ... surrounded by the mob. Her first action was to pick up a child. 'Friends,' she said, 'many of you are mothers. I too am a mother. I am distressed for your children. Is there not something we can do for these innocent little ones? Do you want them to grow up to become real prisoners themselves? Are they to learn to be thieves and worse?' It was in this wise that she reached them. (Whitney 1937 p 152)

And having reached them, one of the first things she did was establish a school for the children, and some time later classes for the mothers too.

We first met Octavia Hill in Chapter 4. She was a nineteenth century housing reformer. She is also sometimes known as the grandmother of social work because of the methods she used when working with poor families. Hill believed that getting to know her 'clients' and their character improved her practice. This gave rise to the concept of 'personal casework'. At the age of 14 she began to help run a Ragged School for children of the poor. Part of the children's 'schooling' was to manufacture goods and sell them.

> Besides being a valuable business apprenticeship, this gave her direct introduction to personal casework. The youngsters were desperately poor, very rough and often vicious. Yet she managed to keep order in the little workshop, mainly by getting to know each one of the children personally as a friend and co-worker. 'I have to study how to interest each,' she said at the time. 'I connect all they say, do, or look, into one whole, I get to know the thing they really care for.' She also made it her business to know their homes and thus began her knowledge of the houses and the family life of the poor. (Young and Ashton 1956: 116)

Later when she began working directly with families and their housing needs, she got first hand experience of what it was like to live in poverty, in poor housing. She did insist that families develop good habits including prompt payment of rent, but she also believed that it was extremely important to establish friendly relationships with tenants. Social casework, she suggested, involved getting to know parents and their children personally.

In her 1869 address to the Social Science Association, Hill said that 'more is meant than whether a man is a drunkard or a woman dishonest, it means knowledge of the passions, hopes and history of people' (quoted in Woodruffe 1962: 52). It means knowledge of character, the inner life and personal experience. In her work with families, she wanted to:

> . . . move, touch and teach them . . . Our ideal must be to promote the happy, natural intercourse of neighbours. Only when face meets face, heart meets heart; only in the settled link with those who are old friends . . . is [there] more opportunity . . . to grow and to shine. (quoted in Woodruffe 1962: 52)

The social work relationship

As we have seen, cognitive, behavioural, problem-solving and solution-seeking approaches relish placing themselves under the evidence-based microscope. And because they are happy to subject all components of what they do to this kind of examination, the 'social work relationship' also falls under their scrutiny. However, it was the American psychologist, Carl Rogers, back in the 1940s who was one of the first to show that there was something about the therapeutic relationship itself, independent of any specific technique, which helped people change.

The way people treat us matters. We are keenly aware of their reactions and responses. I probably wouldn't go back to a hotel where the receptionist was abrupt, not to say dismissive when I ventured to mention that the shower was only offering lukewarm water. My anxieties about the minor operation to remove a small growth are unlikely to go away if the doctor fails to acknowledge my worries about whether or not the lump might be cancerous. A restaurant whose waiters are unsmiling and uncommunicative is unlikely to get my custom again.

The quality of the relationship is particularly important in situations where one party is anxious or angry or distressed. This, of course, is likely to be the case in much of social work practice. All social work theories recognize the importance of the relationship.

However, some practitioners believe that the relationship is the key element. Whereas others might feel that the relationship is the shore from which the techniques of change are launched, the relationship-based practitioner feels that there is no need to look beyond the relationship itself to understand what brings about personal change. It is the quality of the relationship and not any specific technique that determines satisfaction and effectiveness.

Life politics

Relationship-based social work has often been treated unkindly by radical and structural theorists. Traditional radical theories have argued that relationship-based practices are at best a plaster on the deep wound of oppression and at worst a capitalist trick to keep the poor and disadvantaged quiet and in their place.

Chapter 15 outlined the radical social work agenda which seeks to expose the oppression and discrimination suffered by the poor by the rich and powerless. Anthony Giddens (1991) calls this type of work 'emancipatory politics'. That is, the radical social worker seeks to increase equality and raise awareness. The aim is to emancipate those who are poor, oppressed and suffer discrimination so that they can enjoy equal rights, resources and opportunities.

But what happens when emancipation is achieved, either fully or in part? Is this the end of personal need or distress? Do social problems vanish?

The answer is, of course, no. There will still be problems of living – with each other, with ourselves. Couples will fight and argue. There will be child abuse and neglect. A 90-year-old father might antagonize his daughter upon whom he depends for much of his care. Although we might be free of oppression, enjoy equality and escape material want, we are still faced with the challenge and responsibility of how to live our lives, and how to 'be'. Giddens calls these aspirations for living 'life politics'. *Freedom from* injustice and inequality gives us the *freedom to* choose who we want to be and how we want to live (Berlin 1969).

Life politics is about life choices. Who we choose to be is about self-actualization. How we choose to live is about relationships and intimacy. How we take control of the meaning of our own experience is about personal wellbeing and good mental health. But although this freedom is liberating, even exciting, it can also feel stressful. For many of us, the question of how to make life meaningful is unsettling.

Ferguson (2001, 2003a) has translated many of Giddens' ideas for a social work audience. What he shows is that whereas radical social work is rightly concerned with emancipatory politics, life politics requires a different kind of social work, one which values the importance of the relationship.

Today, political life is often much more than tackling inequality. For example, says Plummer (1995), 'the politics of feminism is about the *kinds of lives women choose to live during an emerging era of history*. And with this, inevitably come new ways for men to live too' (p 150, emphasis original). There is a demand for more open, more accurate emotional communication between couples, within families, and among groups. Increasingly, women contemplate a life beyond motherhood. There is also an expectation that men become more involved in care, nurture and family intimacy.

> The net result is a structural transformation in the social organization of intimacy in terms of what Giddens calls the 'pure relationship.' Relationships now tend to be entered into for their own sake, for the rewards that being with another, or other, can bring. (Ferguson 2001: 44)
>
> Enabling the person to (re)gain a sense of mastery over their life needs to be at the centre of social work and life politics . . . It is precisely this mundane, yet radical, concern with enhancing people's mastery that has tended to get lost in social work discourse amidst a critical theory over preoccupied with emancipatory politics and power in its hierarchical forms. (Ferguson 2001: 52)

Interest in the quality of relationships crops up in many areas of social work: adoption; foster care; loss and bereavement; couple counselling; parenting; family life; social care; and mental health. However, in the world of life politics, there is always the danger of relationship breakdown and with it unhappiness, stress, anger, fear and sadness.

When we experience problems in relationships and matters of personal identity, our mental health suffers. We might resort to alcohol or drugs. We might withdraw or become aggressive. Part of the social worker's role is to help service users gain control over what happens to them, to help vulnerable people increase their resilience, to support those in distress as they struggle to get through the day, to improve the politics of daily life and personal experience.

To understand and be understood

When we enter a relationship with another, our mind meets theirs. There is 'intersubjectivity'. The experience can be particularly intense when we are in the throes of love, lost in the joy of a close friendship, or engaged with a highly responsive therapist. We value being understood by others. Friendships, romantic partnerships, and effective working relationships are successful to the extent we connect, mind to mind.

It is human to want to understand and be understood by others. There is a need to be known by others, for them to understand what it feels like to be me, to occupy my world, to have my history, to suffer my anxieties, to recognize my hopes. This is true of service users every bit as much as it is for lovers and friends.

To be alone is a scary place in which to be. The relationship offers the chance to feel safe and be understood. However, past failures and hurts will make most service users cautious. Relationships might not always have served them well. Rejection by parents or physical violence by a partner are likely to have eroded any trust in the value of relationships or any sense that being close to others is a safe place to be. Social workers will have to earn the service user's trust. If they succeed, communication and connection will take place. It is at this point that the relationship has the power to change us.

For self-understanding and change to happen our minds have to be open. As social workers, if we are anxious, or rigid in our practice of a favourite technique, we will not connect with the mind of the other. It is only when practitioners create a space in which the service user feels potentially safe that intersubjectivity occurs and minds engage.

Our mental life continues to be co-created, and to a degree co-regulated, as we relate and interact with others. Our very experience of self is shaped by our relationship with others, just as they are shaped by their relationship with us.

These processes are not smooth. Relationships are a difficult, messy business. But so long as we both continue in the struggle to connect, communicate and understand, there is always the prospect of change, the hope of finding meaning. There is a deep need to be mind-read by the trusted other, just as there is a powerful drive to read the mind of the other. It is in the dynamics of close relationships that our selves form and re-form.

Love and work

Relationship-based social work has been inspired by a number of approaches. Psychodynamic theories, discussed in Chapter 5, remain important. Person-centred and existentialist practices have certainly been influential as we shall see in the next chapter. Attachment theory is central. And over-arching much of what is done in the name of the relationship is a humanistic stance. Humanistic approaches believe that when people are free of constraint and distortion they are motivated to change, grow and seek harmony with those around them. We shall weave a relationship-based approach from these several theoretical threads.

It was Florence Hollis who gave one of the clearest and most forceful expressions of the importance of the relationship in social casework in her classic 1964 book *Casework: A Psychosocial Therapy*. 'Basic to all casework treatment,' she said in the book's second edition, 'is the relationship between worker and client' (Hollis 1972: 228).

In their model of relationship-based practice, Wilson et al (2008: 7–8) propose a number of core characteristics, including:

- each social work encounter is unique;
- human behaviour is recognized as complex; we are made up of both thoughts and feelings that interact consciously and unconsciously making interpersonal life interesting but complicated; and
- placing emphasis on 'the use of self' and the relationship as the means through which relationships are channelled.

Social workers affect and are affected by their clients. They also affect and are affected by their colleagues. One of the major skills of a social worker is to recognize and understand what goes on emotionally when practitioner and service user meet (Howe 2008). Acceptance and understanding, empathy and kindness, attunement and containment are important if service user and worker are to engage and work together.

If we analyze the value of the relationship as described above, two distinct phases can be recognized. The first involves building trust and establishing the relationship.

The second sees the service user beginning to make progress on how best to meet their need or resolve their problem. But you can't even begin the second stage unless the first is firmly in place.

Freud talked of the need to establish love and trust. Only when they have been achieved can 'work' on the problem begin. In similar vein, Bowlby (1988) said that patients first had to feel 'secure' in their relationship with the worker before they could 'explore' their problems and worries.

Social workers therefore have to understand the fundamental importance of the following therapeutic sequence: (i) be warm and friendly, accept and acknowledge, listen and understand, communicate and collaborate, be honest and reliable, and then, and only then; (ii) explore, reflect, analyze, assess, formulate, challenge, criticize, plan, prod, support, encourage, treat, seek meaning and find solutions. Fundamentally:

> *Clients seek to control the meaning of their own experience and the meanings that others give to that experience. Control helps clients to cope, and it empowers.* It boosts self-esteem and personal confidence, and ultimately it encourages people to believe that they are valued and worthwhile human beings. (Howe 1993: 195 emphasis original)

If relationship-based social work has its philosophical roots in humanism, then the most popular and well-known humanistic theory to influence social work is probably the person-centred approach. The theory had its origins in the work of Carl Rogers.

20

Person-centred Approaches

Carl Rogers

Carl Rogers was born in 1902. His family was religious and conservative. It valued hard work. The young Carl was fascinated by nature and the natural sciences. However his interest in people grew steadily stronger and he eventually decided to study clinical psychology. His views became more liberal. This shift wasn't always well-received by his parents. Nevertheless, Rogers felt the changes reflected what he valued. He was gradually cutting himself free from what his parents had wanted and expected of him.

Throughout much of his childhood, Rogers' sense of self-worth had been dependent on what his parents had valued. He felt that if he was to become true to himself he had to overcome the feeling that his worth was conditional on what his parents wanted of him (Hazler 2007: 191).

Rogers concluded that to live inauthentically was to live an unful-filled life. If we feel constrained, trapped and bound by other people's expectations, and if we always feel that we need their approval and acceptance, we can never be our true selves. This is no way to live. It will be a recipe for alienation, irritation and dissatisfaction. If the regard of others is conditional on us behaving as they would like us to behave, we shall live a false life.

The distorting influence of distorted relationships is most damaging during childhood. After all, for young children, parents and family are their whole world. This is where we should be loved unconditionally. But if the regard of our parents is conditional, if we are 'loved' not for ourselves but for how they want us to be, for how we make them feel, we slip the moorings of authenticity. We begin to live an existential lie. We live in a state of bad faith. This is not the road to fulfilment or happiness. Children who are told that only chil-dren who are good or hard-working or grateful deserve parental love, these children grow up not being loved for themselves but for what they do, what they achieve and how they behave.

At odds with ourselves

Without authenticity, the external world and our internal experiences are at odds. How we actually behave and how we should like to be don't coincide. We feel *incongruent*. We find ourselves doing things that we don't like or of which we are not proud, and yet we end up doing them. We experience tension and self-doubt. It is feeling incongruent that also brings clients to counselling, and service users to distress.

Parents who belittle their children for being needy, lovers who become helpless and distressed whenever they feel uncertain about their partner's affection, aging relatives who make sons or daughters feel guilty if they are not prepared to be at their beck and call – these children, partners, sons and daughters experience regard but with heavy conditions attached.

It was while reflecting on the effects that the expectations of his conservative parents had on him that Rogers learned that he must be true to himself and be confident in himself. It is during this period of Rogers' reflections that we also identify some of the key emerging principles of the person-centred philosophy: individuals must rely on themselves, they must become responsible for their actions. We are all strong at heart if only we can free ourselves of guilt, anxiety, anger, and feeling beholden and obliged to please. In order for people to realize their potential, they must learn to define themselves rather than be defined. This line of thinking, of course, isn't too far removed from a strengths-based perspective.

Existentialism

There is a distinct existential tone to much of person-centred thinking. Indeed, throughout the 1930s, '40s and '50s, the emergence of person-centred counselling coincided with a growing interest in existential philosophy.

Existentialists believe that we must recognize that we are free to be and become whoever we choose. We can't blame others for what we do, think and feel. This is to deny personal freedom and responsibility.

We have no 'essential' or determined nature that says that we are condemned to be this way rather than that, to do this rather than that. It's no excuse to say 'I can't help it, I'm just made that way.' Or 'It's all my parents fault; they screwed me up. If it wasn't for them, I wouldn't be so insecure and defensive.' Or 'I'm sorry, I've got to do this. It's more than my job's worth not to.' All these excuses, all these claims that you have no choice are acts of 'bad faith'. In principle, you can always act otherwise. You can choose. You are responsible.

We therefore exist in a state of freedom. Simply to exist is to face endless freedom in all its thrilling glory and all its frightening prospect. In short, existence precedes essence; freedom trumps fate. Whatever constraints we feel under to behave in a certain way, in principle it is always possible to act differently. It may not be easy. It might require us to be brave, to annoy other people, or risk failure, but the option is there.

Existentialism is therefore a philosophy of being and becoming, hence its attraction for some counsellors and therapists. We have the potential to be who we want to be, if only we recognize that we are free, that we can choose. More echoes, here, of strengths, solutions and constructive social work approaches.

Existentialism is a philosophy that demands that we connect with our life and experience. All I really know is my own experience. Only the personal is real, and it is to the experience of my own reality that I must turn and explore if I am to live freely, authentically, and without excuses. If I can connect with this inner experience, my life can be enlarged and enriched. I must free myself of my illusions. I must not be blind to my own freedom. It is at this point that we begin to feel the resonance between existential philosophy and person-centred approaches to helping.

The heady language and the kind of thinking celebrated by person-centred approaches have held a great attraction for many social workers. The appeal to people's inner, subjective experience feels right to those who believe that deep down we all want to be honourable, true, authentic, and complete, whether we are practitioners or service users. We just need to be given a chance.

Self-actualization

If a therapeutic relationship offers a way out of bad faith into a state of freedom and the opportunity to 'actualize' what we believe our true selves to be, then let us provide it. Rogers believed that we have a deep and strong desire to grow and be creative. We long to be independent and free of other people's suffocating control.

Counselling aims to help people free-up their actualizing tendencies and to realize their full potential. Under the right conditions, people will move towards self-regulation and their own enhancement, and away from being controlled by external forces, including other people (Nelson-Jones 1995: 23).

So, in all of us there is an *actualizing tendency*. This tendency provides the energy and motivation to change. The aim of the practitioner is to help the client recognize and then release this energy – to self-actualize (Maslow 1962). Clients and service users have to believe in themselves. They can develop in a positive direction. Every person, believed Rogers, has with himself or herself:

> ... vast resources for self-understanding, for altering his or her self-concept, attitudes, and self-directed behaviour – and that these resources can be tapped only if a definable climate of facilitative psychological attitudes can be provided. (Rogers 1986: 197)

This perspective has given rise to the more generic description of person-centred approaches as 'experiential psychotherapy'. These approaches do not attempt to impose a theoretical explanation on people's experience, which is the case in psychoanalytic, behavioural and cognitive approaches. Rather, the process of simply exploring experience itself is the point of a humanistic approach. It is in that exploration and reflection that we find meaning, purpose and who we are.

However, for this to happen we need to experience a relationship that is free of expectation, one in which there are no conditions. But what might such a relationship look like? How could it help people recognize that they are free and that they have strengths? By subjecting the relationship to scientific scrutiny, Rogers was able to identify what needed to be present in order for a relationship to be experienced as helpful. In 1942 he published the results of these pioneering investigations in his book *Counseling and Psychotherapy*.

The third way

As we have seen, the two dominant psychotherapies in the 1940s were psychoanalytic and behavioural. Psychoanalysts argued the importance of interpretations. Behaviourists developed a range of techniques to get people to change their behaviour. Rogers provided a third way, very different to the existing models of his day.

This 'third force' emphasized creativity, growth and choice (McLeod 1998: 88). People are recognized as purposeful, constructive and self-striving in their search for meaning and fulfilment. Rather than do things *to* the client, the client is credited with the ability to bring about change through his or her own efforts and beliefs.

It is worth reminding ourselves that Rogers was committed to scientific enquiry and evaluation (Rogers 1942, Murdock 2004: 110). He was one of the first therapists to subject his work to objective scrutiny. It was his scientific examination of counselling practice that helped identify what it was about the relationship that brought about therapeutic change. At the time, this empirical approach was in marked contrast to the prevailing psychoanalytic attitude that resisted attempts to examine itself scientifically.

Rogers expressed great confidence in the client. 'This confidence arises,' writes Hazler (2007: 193), 'from a belief that all people have innate motivation to grow in positive ways and the ability to carry out such a growth process'. The basic premise is that people are inherently good. When we are free, we have a natural, in-built tendency to direct ourselves towards a state of wholeness and integration. At heart, and when we are allowed, we all want to be a better person. It therefore follows that clients should be granted a great deal of responsibility for the content, direction and style of the helping relationship. Hence the description 'person-centred.'

Rather than see people driven by unconscious forces (psychodynamic approaches) or shaped by their environment (behavioural approaches), Rogers gave full responsibility back to the individual. If they are helped to free themselves up, people become motivated to take charge of their own lives. They find direction and strength. With freedom and responsibility recovered, clients realize their potential. All this is possible given the right relationship, one in which the counsellor or therapist possesses warmth, empathy and genuineness.

The core conditions

For Rogers, these three qualities – warmth, empathy and genuineness – became the 'core conditions' of the helpful relationship. They were not only necessary, he felt they could be sufficient.

And so we are back to the healing relationship in which all the elements that have been missing are present – the core conditions of unconditional, warm and positive regard; empathy; congruence and genuineness; equality; and collaboration. If present and sustained over time, these elements bring about positive change (Truax and Carkhuff 1967). If we provide the right environment – the therapeutic relationship – people will grow without distortion. There is no need for an assessment. There is no diagnosis. There is no talk of fixed personalities. This is consistent with the belief that we create our own being; we have no essential traits (McLeod 1998: 97). We always have the option to be and do different.

By the 1960s, it was believed by some researchers that so long as the worker possesses these 'core therapeutic conditions' and ensures they are present in the helping relationship, personal change will occur. The counsellor has to create a relationship that will release the client's potential. The effective worker therefore possesses and shows (Gross and Capuzzi 2007):

- Empathy – to see and understand how the world looks and feels from the client's point of view, and *accurately convey that understanding*.
- Respect and positive regard for the other – communicating a belief that the client has the ability to take control of and change his or her own life. We value and respond positively to the love and positive regard of others.
- Genuineness and congruence – the social worker does not play at being a social worker or a helpful person; whatever they do is sincere, authentic and true. Most clients can tell if someone is putting on an act and playing the part.
- Concreteness – the ability of the social worker to tell it like it is, to see the bigger picture, to identify any distortions in the way the client is describing their situation, to help the client be more realistic.
- Warmth – usually communicated through body language including a smile, a touch, a kindly look, a friendly tone of voice.
- Immediacy – the ability to acknowledge and deal with 'here-and-now' factors as they occur in the relationship. The social worker mustn't ignore or avoid the client's anger or fear, sadness or indifference. Remember the relationship and what goes on in it is the subject of interest; it is the medium in which we change.

Much of the time most of us fall short of these saintly virtues. However, the 'use of self' can be developed and improved. Practitioners who are able to critically reflect on what they do and why they do it have a good chance of enhancing their use of the core conditions. They value self-awareness.

The helping relationship, wrote Rogers (1961), is one in which the helper 'has the intent of promoting the growth, development, maturity and improved functioning and improved coping with life of the other' (p 39).

Relationships are where most of us look for comfort and understanding. It is with our friends that we seek pleasure and fun. If we need to pause and reflect, or look for recognition and meaning, it is to others we turn.

Inside experience

Over the years clients have been very clear that the quality of the relationship with the social worker matters enormously (Howe 1993). When clients and service users are asked their views, they tell us that they value social workers who are honest, who are warm and friendly. Even small talk can help establish rapport and a more relaxed atmosphere (de Boer and Coady 2007).

Service users also appreciate practitioners who acknowledge and accept what they are feeling; who don't pass judgement. But this doesn't mean that such practitioners condone, although they do have empathy.

A worker would not for one minute accept that hitting your wife is normal and acceptable. But in response to a man who says that any typical husband would hit a wife who riles him as she does, no amount of arguing that he is wrong and everyone else is right will get him to change his mind. The worker has to 'enter' his mind to see how things look and have got to be this sorry way from his troubled point of view. How has he reached his aggressive conclusion? If his mind can be understood from the inside, it gives the worker clues about how to connect with and then help him re-think and re-value his outlook and assumptions, help him make sense of why he's thinking and acting in such a violent and unacceptable way, and eventually to understand that hitting people who annoy you is neither normal nor acceptable behaviour. It is simply not the right thing to do. If he

we're back in familiar territory having already met many of these ideas in critical theory and the critical social work it has inspired.

The critical reflection process is made up of two stages – analysis and change (Fook 2007: 368). The stage of analysis is one of *de-construction*, of critical reflection. Here, the worker and user become aware of other people's use and mis-use of power. They also become aware of the user's own ideas, thoughts, words and possibilities.

The change stage is one of *re-construction*. It is at this point in the relationship that service users begin to re-value themselves. They begin to develop new ways of seeing their self and their situation. They see the possibility of claiming back power, and with that comes the thrill, and not a little anxiety, of recovering control over the content and meaning of their own life.

The use of self therefore has a number of dimensions: awareness of one's personality traits and belief systems, an understanding of relational dynamics, a recognition of how anxiety intrudes and distorts relationships, and the judicious use of self-disclosure (Dewane 2006).

More modern definitions also insist on the social worker being aware of power imbalances in the worker-user relationship. Power affects the experience and behaviour of both practitioner and service user. So, the social worker needs to ask, or be asked, where does power lie in this relationship, how does it operate, and who is defining the character and direction of what's taking place here (Mandell 2008)?

Payne (2002) offers a nice review of what reflective practice means in social work. The most straightforward version is the simple injunction that practitioners should work with service users in a thoughtful and considered way. Before making decisions or embarking on a course of action, it's important that the social worker considers 'all the angles' and checks 'out all the details before taking the plunge' (Payne 2002: 124). This encourages practice that is not only ruminative but from the service user's point of view, one that is also courteous.

Uncertainty and the reflective practitioner

The most traditional way to be a reflective practitioner is that inspired by the writings of Donald Schön (1983). Practices, including social work, are characterized by uncertainty, complexity and the need to solve problems. They respond best to on-the-job, pragmatic thinking.

In contrast, if you are producing iron or mending cars, once you have worked out the science, engineering and mathematics, all you need is technical know-how. Heat iron ore with coke and lime-stone to 1000°C in a large smelter and blast it with air containing oxygen, and after a while, liquid iron will sink to the bottom ready to be tapped. It happens every time. The process is rational, predictable and technically manageable. But if your work is with people, there is no exact science underpinning what you do.

In the case of social work or counselling or teaching, you need theories and frameworks, but you also need to think on your feet. This involves reflecting on what you have done, why you did it, and what affect it had on you and the service user. Social workers and what they do is so much more fluid and less predictable than, say, computer programming or income tax calculation, which have clear rules governing their production.

Reflection as well as calculation therefore seems much more suited to what social workers do. This is particularly true if the reflec-tion involves the service user who will have his or her own thoughts and feelings about what's happened so far. They might also have ideas about possible ways forward. It's only politicians and managerial control-freaks who think that you can lay down exact rules and pro-cedures for what social workers do and guarantee the outcome.

> Reflection, then, is one of the processes through which clients par-ticipate in social work. We are forced by our experience of their world and problems to *think* carefully about their experiences and respond to them. Social work does not impose a set of prescrip-tions on clients. Instead, it reacts to clients and the world in which they live, and it does so through reflection. (Payne 2002: 127–8 emphasis original)

Time to reflect: Supervision, reflection and emotional availability

More mundane, but equally important is the role that good supervi-sion can play in helping workers develop critical self-awareness. Both one-to-one and group supervision can be of enormous benefit. They create spaces in the day for 'emotional thinking' (Chamberlayne

2004). Good reflective supervision helps a worker deepen her understanding of both her own and the service user's thoughts and feelings. Such 'process' reflection encourages the worker to reflect on what goes on between the self and the service user (Ruch 2005). The value of supervision has long been recognized.

> ... the importance of supervision cannot be over-estimated. It would seem essential, not only for the beginner, but also more senior staff. It is important in the first place because it is a way of sharing the heavy responsibility and anxieties aroused in the course of the work; it is a check against distortion due to personal problems; it is a way of counteracting getting in a rut and it provides an opportunity for learning, to develop and further one's insight and skills. (Saltzberger-Wittenberg 1970: 167)

Together, reflection, reflexivity and supervision aim to increase the worker's emotional and psychological availability for use by the service user. Successful relationships depend on the worker being available and possessing sound social intelligence. These same elements also predict general wellbeing.

22

Wellbeing

Relationship ups and downs

We have seen that social work's nineteenth century pioneers had a clear interest in people. They had a powerful belief that a good relationship can bring about great change, even in those who had fallen on desperate and dissolute times.

The twentieth century witnessed mixed fortunes for those who continued to value the relationship in social work. Some psychodynamic practitioners kept the relationship-flame burning. Behaviourists, while not entirely dismissing the relationship, put technique first. Person-centred and humanistically oriented social workers remained adamant that the relationship is key to good practice.

However, with the rise of managerialist, performance-related, problem-solving, accountability-driven practices that first emerged in the 1980s and continue to the present, there is the danger that the relationship might be seen at best as a luxury and at worst as weak, irrelevant and unscientific.

And that's where relationship-based social work might have rested were it not for the appearance of two most unexpected and unlikely allies: economists and brain scientists. Let's look first at what the economists have to say about the importance of relationships.

Happiness

Over recent years some economists have puzzled over why increasing wealth has not necessarily led to increasing happiness. Certainly, happiness is in short supply when people suffer extreme poverty, poor housing and insufficient food. But once these basics are in place, levels of happiness don't straightforwardly rise with increasing affluence.

For example, over the past 30 to 40 years, levels of happiness have not risen in the UK or USA even though on average people are much better off. In some relatively poor countries, rates of happiness are often much higher than they are in Britain and the States. How can this be?

One of the findings that predicts decreasing happiness, no matter how rich a country is overall, is the wealth gap between rich and the relatively poor. If the gap is very great, average levels of happiness, satisfaction and physical health drop while levels of crime, antisocial behaviour and mental ill health rise (Wilkinson 2000). This also applies to civic trust. The most trusting countries are those with the narrowest range of inequalities (Kohn 2008).

In countries like the UK we have seen the growth of free, unregulated economic markets and a political climate that positively encourages individualism, ambition and competitiveness. With relatively low rates of income tax, this has allowed a small number of people in the financial sector, business, sport, entertainment and the world of celebrity to grow enormously rich. So even though the middle and working classes are also better off, the distance between the top and the bottom in terms of income and wealth has been stretched ever wider.

The emphasis on being responsible for your own success (or failure) in a climate of aggressive, competitive self-interest increases levels of stress. There is always someone who seems to earn and possess far more things than you do. This is a recipe for dissatisfaction and reduced happiness. Although the people at the top of the pile report feeling happy, more and more people feel a relative failure and that the quality of their life is not as good as it might be. ' The wealthy, argues Layard [2005], incite envy in others, spewing out a sort of "social pollution" ' (Weiner 2008: 318).

When economists looked at these findings in more detail, they found that for most people happiness was not only measured in terms of what people earned or possessed, it was also assessed in terms of less tangible goods such as health, relationships and a sense of community. The bonds between people could create a sense of belonging. Living in harmony reduces isolation, anxiety and stress. Added together, these less tangible components predicted people's sense of *wellbeing*.

Psychologists and economists were discovering that so much of people's happiness and wellbeing depended on the quality of their relationships with others. Enjoying respect, being socially involved, and feeling emotionally connected to family and friends, neighbours and colleagues all contributed to wellbeing (Layard 2005, Csikszentmihalyi 1998). The richer, the more dense people's relationships with others, the more happy they tend to be. It's not even the total number of relationships that makes people happy, but the quality and satisfaction their relationships give. These findings provide a powerful boost to the legitimacy and effectiveness of relationship-based social work.

Relationship breakdown

In the late 1970s, as economies shifted towards being more liberal, openly competitive and free market, there was an increasing emphasis on the individual and personal responsibility. In Chapter 11 we saw that self-reliance and self-improvement became the watch words. Making money and increasing your buying power became a major driving force in many people's lives. As many countries moved to the political right, ideas of community, collective action and relationships lost their value. The agenda was one of radical individualism.

The social fabric and the interdependence that previously held people together in communities of interest slowly began to dissolve. So although the increase in freedom released a lot of energy, particularly entrepreneurial energy, it came at a price. In spite of a rise in the standard of living, overall feelings of happiness and wellbeing began to fall.

Social work got caught up in these political and economic changes. We saw in Chapter 11 that the neo-liberals argued that the welfare state was in danger of suffocating people's independence. Many users of social work services, including older people and disabled adults, lacked choice. By its actions, the welfare state confirmed the dependent status of many clients.

It was by introducing free market principles into social work that clients became service users, and personal choice and responsibility increased. Service users could now purchase services. The change from a collective welfare mentality to a liberal, individualistic, free market approach defined service users as rational, independent agents.

But with the freedom to choose came the responsibility to behave well and not interfere with other people's freedoms. If an individual either won't or can't act as a rational agent (say, a parent who abuses their child, or a person suffering paranoid schizophrenia), then the social worker has the statutory right to deny some of their freedoms and impose constraints (see Sheppard 2006).

The rise of free-market economics and their influence on social work was the background against which the ideas of wellbeing unexpectedly came into focus.

Managing social work

At this point I pick up Jordan's important and eloquent analysis of the value of social work and the part it can play in understanding and promoting wellbeing (Jordan 2007). He reminds us that the material economy produces physical goods and services. Thinking this way allows you to measure services, set targets, and assess performance and productivity.

It was the liberal thinkers who began to apply free-market principles and the management-speak that went with it to social work. Social workers were constrained to do only those things that could be measured: setting targets for the number of children who are adopted, having a check-list for the number of support services purchased by an 80-year-old service user, providing a 4 week social skills training programme for a man with learning difficulties.

Social work was also being broken down into component parts. Each part was carried out by a different person rather than just one person in a continuous relationship with the service user. Assessments might be carried out by one team of workers, while support and interventions were carried out by another. Often only one person does the direct face-to-face work with a service user but she has little control over the content and direction of that work which is determined and managed by someone else. Another worker might specialize in reviews.

> As a consequence of all this, practice has become a hectic round of assessment, risk-management and review. It has become rather formalised, arm's length and office-based, involving check-lists and standardised procedures. (Jordan 2007: 44)

In this world, less tangible practices that can't easily be quantified and counted, such as a long term relationship, are gradually eased out of the social work repertoire.

The interpersonal economy and social capital

But so much of life is more than buying and measuring things. It is many of the things that are so difficult to target or measure that actually improve our feelings of worth and wellbeing. These include close relationships, feeling emotionally supported, belonging to a group, feeling part of a community. Jordan (2007) calls these experiences the 'interpersonal economy'.

The quality of our interpersonal world determines our emotional wellbeing. Since the mid-nineteenth century, the world of relationships and personal interdependence has been the stuff of social work. Social work seen in this way is a moral enterprise. It involves two or more people who meet to see how life can be made to feel better.

What has happened since the late 1970s is that many liberal, capitalist economies have put the emphasis on freedom, individuality and personal responsibility. This has improved material productivity and increased national wealth. However, it has decreased overall levels of happiness and wellbeing. And because social work has been subject to the same changes that have led to performance, target-driven, micromanaged practices across all the health, welfare, educational and justice services, it lost faith in the value of relationship-based practices.

The rediscovery of the link between the quality of personal relationships and wellbeing by economists and psychologists has therefore come at an interesting time for social work. Doubt has been cast:

> ... on the fundamental assumption behind the policies of both neoliberal and Third Way governments that putting more money in people's pockets, so they can choose the particular bundle of goods and services they prefer, is more important than providing a good overall context for their lives together. (Jordan with Jordan 2000: 5)

The bonds that people have with others add up to what sociologists and economists call 'social capital'. The richer these bonds, the higher the social capital. The higher the social capital, the lower the level of stress. Low levels of stress and a feeling of being socially embedded raise happiness, boost wellbeing, reduce crime and improve health.

Social workers, particularly those who base their practices on ecological, community development and strengths-based approaches have long held an interest in the notion of social capital (Garbarino and Kostelny 1993, Jack 2000, Saleebey 1997, 2001). They recognize that communities that enjoy dense social networks of family life, friendships, neighbourliness, shops, pubs, play groups, youth centres, schools, informal support groups, and leisure facilities tend to have more stable, content and problem-free individuals. People value and enjoy the social bonds and feelings of trust that bubble up spontaneously in such communities.

A powerful way, therefore, to reduce rates of isolation in old age, anti-social behaviour, child abuse and neglect, and mental health problems is to promote social capital. Ecological and community developmental models of social work can show you the way forward.

The return of the relationship

This argues not just for relationship-based casework but also relationship-based community work. These practices can improve the quality of interactions between people at the level of family, group, neighbourhood and community.

Social work is about promoting *inter*dependence, not independence. Good relationships engender respect and a sense of belonging. They encourage commitment. 'People *create value* in their interactions' (Jordan 2007: 12 emphasis original).

Relationships are where people experience subjective feelings of wellbeing. Children and adult care services should be about the promotion of long term interdependency – the interpersonal economy – and not a series of one-off experiences with different social care workers (for example, see Jack 1997). And so, concludes Jordan:

> Social work is primarily a relationship which is about relationships, in their broadest sense – with fellow citizens as well as partners, families, friends and kin. Its value must be understood in terms of the interpersonal economy. (Jordan 2007: 19–20)

Social workers should help service users enter into dialogue and communication – with the worker, between family members, with health and welfare agencies, between neighbours, and across communities. It is in the context of honest, accurate and meaningful conversation that understanding, worth and change are accomplished. It is in the taking part that esteem and belief occur.

Thus, social work is as much about the way social workers do it as it is about what they do. The manner of practice matters as much, if not more than its technical content. 'The relationship always comes first,' says Kunip, a Thai school principal discussing happiness with Eric Weiner (2008: 291). 'It is more important than the problem.'

The relationship, therefore, is more than the vehicle that delivers the service or that facilitates the technique. It is the agent of change itself. Well, that's what the economists are beginning to say. But what can the brain scientists tell us?

23
Brains for Social Workers

Use it or lose it

Faith in the value of the relationship has been kept by counsellors and social workers with humanistic leanings. However, the importance of the relationship, for psychological health and development, has now been recognized by scientists who study the brain. It is the neurosciences that are beginning to transform our understanding of the importance of human relationships and the part they play in development and wellbeing. In order to see why, first we need to take a short detour.

The human brain contains 100 billion neurons, or nerve cells, each connected by synapses to thousands of other neurons. There are therefore trillions of possible neural pathways and connections making the human brain the most complex thing in the known universe. Understanding how the brain works in general, and developing a theory of the brain in particular is one of the most exciting challenges that scientists face in the twenty first century.

At birth, babies have a huge amount of learning and development ahead of them. Much of the 'hard-wiring' of the brain takes place in the earliest years of development (Gerhardt 2004). Although many of the basic functions of the brain are in good working order at birth, including those that regulate body temperature and deal with digestion, other higher order functions only become organized gradually over the first few months and years of life.

Even more intriguing is the realization that the brain is a self-organizing developmental structure. Key to understanding much of the brain's early development is the finding that the majority of nerve cells or neurons *are programmed to make sense of experience but they need exposure to experience before they can make sense of it.*

I'm almost tempted to repeat that last, slightly odd sounding sentence. What it means is that different parts of the brain are sitting there expecting to process and make sense of all manner of things – what we see and hear, what we think and feel, the way we deal with stress, the acquisition of language, the ability to control our muscles and the movements they allow. But before they can process and make sense of these many things, they must first be exposed to and experience them.

For example, it is only when the brain is exposed to visual stimuli that it learns to process and make sense of the nerve signals that come via the eyes and optic nerves. In other words the brain (specifically, the occipital lobes at the back of our heads) learns to see by learning to process visual stimuli. It learns to integrate all the component bits of vision including colour, contrast, shape, orientation, perspective, texture and movement. Only then do we see the external world as bright, colourful, vibrant and seamless.

It is during this exposure to visual experience that the infant's brain cells, the ones sitting there waiting to deal with visual information, begin to develop rich, busy, complex connections with each other as they learn to process and make sense of the visual experience. In effect, exposure to visual experience helps the neurons in the visual processing parts of the brain become 'hard wired' to each other, forming complex neural networks. Or as Donald Hebb (1949) famously put it, 'cells that fire together, wire together'.

Those infant brain cells that don't get stimulated during these early sensitive periods of brain development don't develop synaptic connections with other brain cells. They die off in a process known as 'pruning'. Or as Hebb again neatly said, neurologically speaking, 'use it or lose it.'

In short, neurons that are programmed to make sense of an experience but which don't get exposed to that expected experience don't develop. Without the expected stimulation the neurological connections don't develop.

Thus, there are sensitive periods during children's development when the brain is expecting to experience a whole variety of sensory stimuli. Once the sensitive phase has passed, it's more difficult for the brain to recover and make these connections. A child who has missed out on a particular sensory stimulation or set of experiences during these sensitive periods will have difficulty processing and making sense of that set of experiences once she has passed the key developmental stage for that function.

For example, a seriously neglected child who has not been exposed to language and who has been deprived of conversation, will have difficulty developing language. Even if such a child is removed at a later age and placed in a rich language environment, say with skilled foster carers, the child may still have language problems even years later. Some recovery is likely but children who have missed out on language experience during their early years still have problems. Their brains just haven't developed the neurological hard-wiring to process and make sense of language with any great fluency.

In the case of extremely neglected children, such as the notorious case of Genie (Rymer 1994), recovery tends to be most marked in terms of acquiring a vocabulary, but problems still remain with grammar.

On 4 November 1970, a young, badly neglected girl was discovered by the Los Angeles police. She was 13 years old but looked only six. Since being a toddler, she had been locked alone in a single room by her father. During the day he strapped her to a potty-chair. At night he tied her into a sleeping bag. He rarely spoke to her. Her mother, who suffered very poor sight and was very frightened of her husband, was forbidden to see her daughter. This was a case of extreme social, sensory and language deprivation. Genie suffered a range of physical, cognitive and developmental impairments, including major language deficits. Although she received intensive support and help once she was placed with foster carers, Genie's language, in spite of some improvements, remained relatively simple and child-like.

Nevertheless, in spite of these catch-up problems, the optimistic thing to note is that some recovery is possible. The brain remains 'plastic'. In other words, although the early years are crucial, the brain retains some ability to neurologically organize and re-organize itself throughout the lifespan. It's never too late.

The social brain and the social self

Perhaps one of the more interesting things to emerge from all this brain science research is how the psychological, emotional and social self form.

The same principles apply. In order for children to develop social skills, emotional intelligence and the ability to reflect on their own and other people's mental states, they need to be exposed to good quality social, emotional and reflective experiences. They get all of this whenever they interact and relate with sensitive and attuned parents, older family members, teachers, and any other responsive, psychologically available adults.

The quality of children's early attachment relationships with their primary carers seems particularly important. The effect of early attachment relationships on children's emotional, social and neurological development has been of especial interest to developmental neuroscientists.

Attuned and responsive relationship experiences are handled by various parts of the brain, particularly the limbic system (sometimes known as the emotional centre of the brain) and the front of the brain situated above the eyes (known as the right prefrontal cortex). The limbic system processes emotional experiences. The prefrontal cortex helps us to make sense and consciously reflect on emotions and the relationships in which so many of our strongest feelings arise.

The richer the quality of children's relationship and emotional experiences the more the brain has the opportunity to develop dense and highly integrated neurological structures connecting the limbic system and the pre-frontal cortex. This allows children to process and make sense of the extraordinary complex business of relating with other people.

The more sense children can make of their own and other people's mental and social lives, the more skilled they become at social relationships. They develop good social understanding. They enjoy emotional intelligence. But you need high order brain power to do all of these complicated social and emotional things.

Children who suffer impoverished or traumatic relationships in which there is deficient, disturbed or distorted emotional communication find that their brain development is compromised. These neurological deficits are particularly noticeable in the areas that are supposed to process social information and make sense of emotions and other people's mental states.

If you find it difficult to monitor and make sense of your own and other people's thoughts, feelings and behaviour you will find relationships stressful and difficult. You might also have mental health problems. Many mental health problems occur because people find it difficult to regulate their emotions. Anxiety disorders, depression, fears and phobias, anger and aggression are just a few examples.

The more problems you have in processing and regulating both your own and other people's feelings and behaviour, the more you deny yourself the opportunity to experience good quality, two-way, responsive relationships. Other people will find you hard going. A vicious circle sets in. Those who need good quality, emotionally attuned relationships the most are least likely to experience them.

Engaging minds

But what happens if you do eventually experience a sensitive, attuned relationship with another person? Can the brain recover? Can it get better at processing and making sense of the self and other people emotionally, psychologically and socially?

The encouraging answer to these questions is yes. Neuroscientists have shown how the brain can 're-wire' itself when it experiences good, rich, well-modulated two-way psychological stimulation in the context of a relationship. Recovery is not quite so easy for children who have suffered extreme trauma and neglect from a very young age and for a long time, but even in these cases, some psychosocial progress can be achieved when the children are placed with new responsive carers.

It therefore seems that a good relationship can heal. In his book *The Neuroscience of Psychotherapy: building and re-building the human brain* (2002), Louis Cozolino explains that therapeutic relationships provide a rich environment that allows the growth and integration of neural networks.

With improved neurological communication between the emotional and social processing parts of the brain, feelings of stress can be regulated. People cope better. Their social understanding increases. Relationships run more smoothly thus providing ever more responsive and attuned experiences.

A benign circle sets in. If poor relationships in the early years are where neurological development falters, then good relationships later on in life are where neurological recovery is likely to take place.

Neurologically speaking, relationship-based social work has the capacity to nurture and revive (Cozolino 2002, Applegate and Shapiro 2005). As far as brain scientists are concerned, trusting and emotionally attuned relationships really do help.

Self-organizing developmental structures

We learned on the opening page of this chapter that the brain is a self-organizing developmental structure, particularly in the early years of its growth. This means that not only is it genetically programmed to learn from experience, it needs exposure to experience in order to develop the capacity to process and make sense of the very experiences to which it needs exposure.

All of this delicious and delightful science in which there are feedback loops and the potential for endless adaptations, new understandings, and exquisite attunements between our senses, our brains and our ability to understand both ourselves, others and the world around us resonates rather nicely with many of the ideas put forward by critical theorists and reflexive practitioners discussed in Chapters 16 and 21. The recursive nature of our neurological, psychological and interpersonal life explains much of our ability to adapt and move forward. Having formed and taken our psychological shape in the context of close relationships, our ability to change and re-form in the context of close relationships begins to make sense.

Although taking its cue from critical theory rather than the modern neurosciences, the idea of a 'critical best practice' represents a form of social work that attempts to generate a practice out of the very constituents of the worker-service user encounter itself. There is no fixed blue-print, just a philosophical stance out of which an attuned practice develops and evolves. Critical best practice will be the last theory we consider in this book before I round off with some concluding thoughts.

24
Critical Best Practice

Negotiating uncertainty and weaving realities

We have seen that over recent years there has been a growing mood to combine formal theory *and* the wisdom gained from practice *with* what service users have to say.

Such is the uncertainty and messiness of real day-to-day social work that a 'best practice' can only be achieved by being alert, attuned, reflective, research aware, critically minded, creative and flexible. In response to the constantly shifting dynamics of the relationship between the social worker and service user, it just isn't possible to guarantee or predict quite how things are going to turn out. On top of the uncertainty built into the worker-user relationship are the ever present influences and views of families, neighbours, communities, social work agencies, health professionals, teachers, police officers, judges, journalists, and politicians.

Of course, the social worker can't help but have ideas about what is going on, but she has to do much of her thinking on her feet. If she is to think well and reflect clearly, she must strive to listen, respect, discuss, negotiate, understand, suggest, disagree, try out, change her mind, be honest and be curious.

A critical best practice

The idea of a 'critical best practice' in social work is described in a book edited by Jones, Cooper and Ferguson (2008). Their work draws a number of threads together. Their approach contains elements of critically reflective, solution-focused and strengths-based practices.

Ferguson (2003b, 2008) offers a helpful outline of what is 'best practice' social work. First, social workers must try to understand the service user's experience and the meaning it has for him or her.

Practitioners must tune into the service users' 'subjective experience' as they tell their story, their 'narrative' (Ferguson 2003b: 1011).

There is a critical and reflective use of self by the social worker. There is an awareness of the part that the emotional and psychological condition of both the service user and social worker play in the relationship.

The practitioner keeps an open mind. It is important to hear the service user's voice which for so long has been silenced by the roar of the expert. As Bauman (1992) also argues, postmodern stances seek to give marginal groups a voice. It is the job of the social worker to interpret one group to another, to make the unfamiliar familiar, to make those who are socially different feel understood and less threatening. The aim is to accept and live with difference and diversity. The hope is to promote tolerance.

Social workers try to understand what is going on in a particular situation and with an individual service user. In this approach, social workers resist: 'prescriptive, evidence-based approaches and single methodologies. The argument here is not that the knowledge and research base of professional expertise is unimportant, but rather that the context within which knowledge and skills are exercised is unique to specific situations and individuals.' (Jones and Powell 2008: 56)

At this level, social work is an inexact science. There are just too many variables to be entirely sure of where a person, a family or a relationship will be this time next week. Unexpected things happen that catapult cases in unexpected directions. People get drunk. Old people fall over and break their bones. Police officers arrest people who also happen to have a mental illness. Mothers abandon their children. Bailiffs remove all of a family's furniture.

Unknown unknowns

These inherent states of uncertainty, unpredictability and complexity are a feature not just of social work's concerns, but they also characterize economics, politics and many other applied social sciences. Taleb (2008), a writer, economist and philosopher, calls such matters 'black swan events'.

It was the belief of people in mediaeval Europe that all swans were white. By calling something a 'black swan', the medieval mind implied that the thing couldn't exist, it would never happen. But then in the seventeenth century, explorers visiting Australia found swans that were indeed black. Black swans had simply never been predicted. The impossible had happened.

Taleb's argument is that lurking on the close horizon, there are always unknown and unexpected things waiting to happen. No matter how good our intelligence, we never see them coming. They are the famous 'unknown unknowns' of Donald Rumsfeld, the one time American Defence Secretary.

The global financial crisis of 2008, triggered by banks creating ever more tenuous financial systems and funding sub-prime loans to buy houses by people who run a higher than average risk of not being able to keep up their mortgage repayments, is a good example of a 'black swan event'. No-one saw the crisis coming, particularly one on such a scale. All the fancy theories, economic tools and models of risk management analysis used by bankers and financiers proved useless in predicting a rare, but devastating event. It turned out that they were no better than astrologers when it came to predicting the financial future of the global market.

Admittedly on a much smaller scale, chance matters and unpredictable events happen in everyday social work as they do in economics and finance. Statham and Kearney (2007) agree:

> Uncertainty and complexity are at the centre of social work because it specializes in situations where there are no known solutions ... It is important to understand that this is the nature of the social work task not an unfortunate consequence of it. For this reason, social work can never be a technical activity based simply on assessment formats, models or methods. (p 102)

So, we need theories to give us a context and to help us keep our bearings. We can never be complacent. We have to be flexible and open-minded. Whatever the ups and downs, we have to stay with service users. We have to create meaning, or literally our practice becomes meaningless. It is by staying with people at times of need and difficulty that the roller coaster gradually slows down. The highs and the lows begin to even out so that the casework ride becomes less disturbing, more manageable.

In spite of their limitations and provisional nature, theories represent some of the best, most thought-through ideas that we have about people, society and relationships. Theories therefore help construct meaning. If we come across as 'meaningful' to service users, there is the hope that a conversation can take place. Social worker and service user learn to connect and engage. A relationship forms in which meaning can be addressed, discussed, negotiated and re-defined. Once more we see that service users have the opportunity to control the meaning of their own experience and the meaning that others give to that experience.

Of course, there is always and inevitably a political context within which social work takes place that also affects what it means. The presence of power has to be recognized. Contradictions and tensions abound as practitioners juggle with issues of respect, danger, risk, harm, safety, partnership, care, protection, equality and loss of freedom.

But whatever the needs and concerns, social workers have to ask themselves 'what has worked well, what is of value?' Critical best practice 'identifies 'what is best and most successful as a means for moving forward?' (Preskill and Coghlan 2003 p 1 quoted in Ferguson 2008: 33). It hinges on being empathic and engaging with people's stories. It demands careful listening. Expert solutions seem to make it nervous.

In the end, social work takes its shape and character as it puzzles over and struggles to make sense of what's going on, and as it tries to find ways forward. Ferguson (2008) cites the edited work of Pease and Fook (1999) to make the same point:

> There are many perspectives and voices and it is now recognized that they all need to be heard if the complex nature of 'truth' is to be established. (p 21)

The crooked path of practice

When working with service users in a critical and reflective way, the path of intervention is rarely straight. It twists. It turns back on itself before moving off again in a different direction. Outcomes simply cannot be predicted. There are no blueprints for practice (Jones and Powell 2008: 67). The best we can do is travel with care, curiosity and compassion as we accompany and guide service users on uncertain journeys to more meaningful and stress-free futures.

All of this is nicely rendered by Jones and Powell (2008) in their account of working with Amelia, a woman in her early 80s, diagnosed with Alzheimer type dementia, and living alone in a council house. She received some support from her cousin, Bob, who was in 60s and had never been particularly close to Amelia. He had his own family and children. The original referral implied that Amelia was no longer capable of living independently and that residential care was probably most appropriate. Bob, at least in the first instance, supported this plan.

However, the social worker – Imogen – began her involvement with a long, careful phase of trying to understand Amelia by listening to the story of her life. It soon became apparent that her current home was a source of comfort and a place of security. What home meant for Amelia, not just physically but psychologically, had to be the starting point of any best practice. Sensing Imogen's growing understanding, Amelia slowly began to develop a relationship of trust with the social worker.

> By accepting the importance of Amelia's home and neighbourhood, Imogen was able to gradually negotiate community-based support options, which would enable Amelia to remain in her own home as she strongly wished to do. These included local day care, home care and the support of a volunteer from an organisation for older people . . . What is particularly impressive is the level of understanding which Imogen developed from really attending to an individual's story. Amelia was much less suspicious of support options which emerged from her own story, within a carefully developed relationship of trust, than she was of previous attempts by health professionals to impose care solutions. (Jones and Powell 2008: 59)

Imogen knew that as Amelia's dementia progressed, things would have to change, but she was prepared to go at Amelia's pace. She maintained a relationship with Amelia that allowed for constant negotiation and re-negotiation as needs and context changed. It gradually became apparent that Amelia, who was possibly beginning to hallucinate, was feeling less and less secure at home. It was Amelia, who for so long had resisted residential care, who eventually agreed it was the place where she now felt most safe.

By staying with Amelia, moving at her pace and remaining in touch with her feelings about her changing capacities, the social worker facilitated a relatively smooth and sensitive transition from independence without support, to independence with support, before the final move to residential care.

Imogen got inside Amelia's story and as a result her practice was attuned, sensitive and effective. There was no single theory, policy or piece of legislation guiding the overall case. Rather, having understood the world as experienced by Amelia, Imogen could draw on different ideas, supports and resources at different times.

Imogen resisted being drawn into worrying about the risks involved. Instead, she tried to see the world from Amelia's point of view. Imogen's responses were therefore shaped by Amelia's needs rather than the risks expressed by health and social care managers. The social worker:

> ... sought out Amelia's voice and placed it at the centre of the assessment ... This is social work which resists the notion of assessment as a one-off event and engages imaginatively with complexity and change. It demands of practitioners the confidence not to be reduced to inaction by the recognition of uncertainty and contradiction, but to act compassionately on the basis of critical analysis. (Jones and Powell 2008: 68)

Practice is an untidy, unpredictable business. The best that social work can do is to be wise about this uncertainty and complexity. Although no one theory can ever explain everything, each one tells us something. We have to remain puzzled and interested.

The form of social work

Looking back over the years, although theoretical fashions change, there is an uncanny familiarity about what social workers are doing today when they meet service users and what social workers did 40 years ago when I began my professional career.

Indeed, when you read accounts of social work practice written 60, 80, 100 or more years ago, again, they feel and sound stubbornly familiar. This doesn't mean that new ideas aren't being incorporated into practice. Rather, these ideas get woven into the more densely textured fabric of the actuality of day-to-day practice, though rarely in a pure, unadulterated form.

Is this because what social workers do is too complex to submit to single truths and stand-alone techniques? Or is there something about the social work encounter that makes it inherently uncertain and unfixed, hence the need for adaptive thinking, negotiated meaning and flexibility of mind? The critical social theorist would have no hesitation is answering 'yes' to the last question. There is no magic bullet. There is no single theoretical truth.

And the reason for recognizing that social work practice is inherently unpredictable and possessed of uncertainty is that it lives in a world of language, relationships, meaning and interpretation. None of these can be unambiguously fixed. Meaning has to be negotiated. As the social worker speaks, interprets and acts, the service user in turn listens, speaks, perceives, thinks, feels, reacts and makes her own interpretations, carries out her own actions. Language and its interpretation is the medium in which most social work takes place. The social work relationship is therefore a dynamic, recursive, reflexive place. The reflexive character of social work explains both its uncertainty and its perennial familiarity.

Perhaps all of this is beginning to sound rather lofty and abstract, but it is not a million miles away from what any good relationship is like, say between friends, lovers, or colleagues.

We monitor and interpret what we feel, think, say and do and what the other feels, thinks, says and does. We're also aware that they are doing exactly the same. In the middle of all this, we struggle to understand and be understood. There are moments when all seems clear, only for muddle and fog to cloud the conversation a moment later. But we continue in our efforts to understand and be understood. We want to connect. And so we stutter on. This is the nature of communication. It characterizes even the best relationships. It certainly captures what it feels like to be with service users as we listen to their needs, hear their distress, and describe our role and express our concerns. The relationship tries to be honest and open. There must be recognition and respect. And above all, informing all that we do is that defining trinity of care, compassion and curiosity.

The meaningful relationship

At the centre of all this communication and reflexivity is the social worker-service user relationship. The relationship acts as a constant.

Its obstinate presence has been found in the practices of social work's founders – Octavia Hill, Elizabeth Fry, Mary Richmond. It is a central feature of Florence Hollis's psychosocial casework. Task centred and cognitive-behavioural practitioners are absolutely clear that their skills and techniques depend for their success on establishing a good working relationship with the service user. Critical and reflexive approaches recognize that language both carries and is carried by the relationship. Psychodynamic and person-centred social workers put the relationship at the heart of their practice. Applied attachment theory is fundamentally and critically a relationship-based practice. Wilson et al (2008) and Hennessey (forthcoming) set the relationship at the heart of their ideas.

The central role given to the relationship by so many theories might go some way to explaining why social work has a curiously familiar, unchanging look to it, decade after decade. It might also explain why it has never wholly succumbed to a dominant paradigm. In their time, both radical and cognitive-behavioural social workers have bemoaned the profession's apparent failure to embrace fully the self-evident truths of their theoretical virtues, but maybe they are missing the point.

It isn't that social workers are being obtuse, wilfully resistant or peculiarly dense that they fail to see the brilliance of an evidence-based this or an ideologically correct that. If behavioural or radical or solution-based social work were so obviously the answer, it would be perverse of social workers in the extreme to ignore the prospect of guaranteed success.

No, the shape and character of social work, the thing that makes it perennially the same, is that it forms and takes its shape from the centre outwards. The centre is the relationship. It is where minds meet, communication happens, and language and meaning are traded.

When the social worker meets the service user a number of things have to happen. She must connect, be empathic, and seek understanding. The service user wants to be understood. There must be a search for meaning. And with understanding and meaning comes control, the recovery of hope, the build up of resilience, the ability to cope.

These strengths and solutions can be sought via any one of a range of theoretical approaches. For example, many of the skills and treatment techniques, say of the cognitive-behaviourist or task-centred worker, will facilitate connection and understanding. However, the choice of theory and technique is established in dialogue, critically and reflexively. The approach taken at any one time might be peculiar to a particular worker-user relationship depending on the knowledge base of the worker and the personality of the service user, but the reality fashioned is theirs.

> Approaching knowledge as situated does not deny the possibility of social truths. We can only know the social world from a specific vantage point. Our standpoint makes knowledge possible. It also means our social ideas are always perspectival; we must give up the idea of a total, comprehensive type of social knowledge. Social truths are always one-sided, both revealing and obscuring social reality. If we approach knowledge as situated, we should also be attentive to the ways that knowledge shapes our behaviour and social life. Knowledge is not only about representing reality but about making and constructing reality. (Seidman 2004: 279)

As social workers, we construct workable realities with our service users, taking advantage of whatever is to hand and what makes people feel comfortable, engaged, trusting, understood, purposeful, in control and hopeful.

The beating heart at the centre of practice is the relationship. It involves the use of self, respect, sensitivity, empathy, curiosity, intersubjective awareness, and the search for meaning and understanding. It is the vehicle that helps minds connect and engage. Trusting the social work relationship can be difficult for those who are anxious or angry, tired or desperate, suspicious or depressed. But the desire is there and it is up to the social worker to facilitate it. Only when the relationship is realized can the cognitive-behavioural or task-centred, solution-focused or critically best practitioner begin business.

25
The Best in Theory

Good social work and best practice

In passing, we noticed that 'critical best practice' is a little suspicious of an over-emphasis on entirely evidence-based social work. I'm not sure we can be quite so dismissive. The trouble is, though, that any reconciliation between social work's more entrenched theories is difficult as each believes that to admit too much interest in the ideas of the other is to sup with the devil, or at least to find oneself in a conceptually untenable position.

Examples are legion. Evidence-based practitioners don't have much time for traditional psychoanalytic theories. If they bother at all, radical and structural approaches only describe cognitive-behavioural social work the better to criticize it. Solution-oriented practitioners simply can't condone problem-solving approaches; for them to start with the problem is the problem. Critically reflexive practitioners feel uncomfortable with the idea that the social worker is the expert and the sole repository of treatment knowledge and skills; it is too one-sided and disempowering.

We could go round in circles describing how each theory in turn is intent on shooting another until there is no theory left standing. If we remain rigid, avoiding theoretical slaughter on this scale is not going to be conceptually easy. However, I propose to take a softer, more accommodating, albeit conceptually less rigorous view. This may end up pleasing no-one but it might reflect something of the character of social work. The position adopted recognizes that some elements of some social work theories have much stronger claims on practice than others, and these I shall support. In order to get us into this way of thinking, we need to have a longer look at this word 'best', as in 'best practice'.

It seems obvious that social workers should practice all that is 'best'. But 'best' in what sense? 'Best' has a number of meanings, some quantitative and some qualitative.

Best scores

Achieving the best score in an archery competition simply means gaining the most points. The best runner would be one who wins his races. Getting the best price for an object depends whether you're selling or buying. Sellers want the highest price; buyers want the cheapest. 'Best value' objects suggest that the buyer feels that for the money spent, she's got the best quality available in that price range.

Claiming that this procedure is the best treatment for your illness suggests that it is the one most likely to cure you and bring you back to health. If the treatment is administered by a doctor, you would quite properly expect that she could, if asked, produce research evidence supporting the claim that, indeed, the treatment given is the best, the most effective. The evidence, obtained by carefully designed, conducted and evaluated research, should tell the doctor what works.

These examples of recognizing the 'best' are quantitative in nature. Talking of 'best practice' in social work can conjure one or more of these quantitative measures. Some managers might want social workers to be efficient in terms of numbers of clients seen, the time spent with them, and the cost per contact or service provided.

However, the most familiar quantitative interpretation of best practice social work is akin to the medical example given above. Put simply, is what social workers do effective, and is there evidence to prove it? In the UK, the Social Care Institute for Excellence (SCIE) has been set up to answer this very question, and thereby promote an evidence-based practice.

In language typically direct and uncompromising, Sheldon and Macdonald (2009) argue as follows:

> what works for whom, at what cost, in what circumstances, over what time-scale, against what outcome indicators, how, and why?' should surely be the main preoccupation of training courses for social workers. All other values and ethics considerations, however exciting to debate, are marginal unless such concerns predominate. (p 89)

Their argument is robust, powerful and takes no prisoners. They go on to say that:

> theories are *not* created equal. Some are more systematically arrived at on the basis of more and better empirical evidence; some are frankly fanciful . . . If some theories prove more valid and reliable than others that are less testable, then the latter must be relegated. (Sheldon and Macdonald 2009: 54, emphasis original)

The challenge implied in these quotes demands that social work academics, trainers and practitioners give the arguments for an evidence-based practice some very serious thought and attention. The case the authors make for an evidence-based practice is well made, and nicely spiced with their undisguised exasperation that many in the profession still pursue theories that are 'frankly fanciful'.

Social work that values research and evidence-based practice therefore rules in some theories and rules out others. Ruled in are cognitive-behavioural approaches, large chunks of task-centred work, some applications of attachment theory, and those elements of relationship-based practice that help create a therapeutic alliance, a necessary, but on this analysis, not a sufficient condition. Possibly promising, but still light on research evidence supporting their effectiveness and therefore still largely unproven, are strengths-based perspectives, brief solution focussed therapies, and some types of family therapy.

Best quality

However, there are other uses of the word 'best' that get us into different conceptual fields. This is the best meal I've ever had. I'll give you the best possible care. That's the best looking boat in the harbour. She's the best painter in the class. These are judgements of taste, of beauty. They tend to involve the senses. Although there may be some agreed sense of what constitutes beauty or skill, there is a large element of subjectivity in these judgements.

These more qualitative, subjective versions of best practice in social work might allow in other types of theory. These aesthetics of practice might lead to the idea of 'social work as art' argued so originally by Hugh England (1986).

We might turn to the judgements of clients and service users and ask them what they think constitutes best practice. Service users might express great satisfaction with the help or support they've received. Clients might be content with relationship-based practices if they evaluate the experience as comforting, reassuring, revelatory and satisfactory. A disfigured life might well appreciate the beauty of simply being understood by another. Reflexive approaches are keen to involve service users in determining the definition and direction of practice. Again, this philosophy might please the normally powerless service user.

By their nature, radical and structural practices are more difficult to judge quantitatively. These approaches seek to change the political, social and economic climate with a view to improving the lot of service users. In this sense, best practice implies a notion of the good society, what it looks like and how it might be achieved. Not surprisingly, this is politically contested ground. More conservative observers might judge the success of a radical structural intervention as 'worst' practice.

The best course of action

There is, though, a third way of thinking about what is best. It involves both quantitative and qualitative evaluations, the sciences and the humanities. It crops up in situations when we're not entirely sure what to do. There are many situations in life when it's not immediately obvious what should happen next. We might ask 'what is the best thing to do?' If you're out walking in a remote area and your companion stumbles and breaks her ankle, you will wonder: 'What is the best course of action?'

In situations of this kind, you will need to take stock and make an assessment. You will need to gather as much information as you can in order to make an analysis. Information gathering, assessment and analysis in this sense are quantitative exercises. But they don't always tell you what to do. This requires a qualitative assessment. It needs a judgement.

In 1739, David Hume, the Scottish philosopher, famously argued that it is not possible to argue from an *is* to an *ought*. What '*ought* to be' does not follow from 'what *is*'. Descriptive statements of themselves can't lead to prescriptive statements. No matter how much is known factually about a situation, the facts don't tell you what you ought to do. What ought to be done requires a judgement. Judgements are moral matters. They require different arguments, other kinds of reasoning. Ethical thinking is involved. Values come into play.

A description of poverty and poor housing, in itself, does not prescribe a redistribution of wealth or the overthrow of capitalism. It doesn't straightforwardly follow from the proposition that a parent's care of her children *is* neglectful that her children *ought* to be removed and placed in public care. An ethical case has to be made to re-distribute wealth or remove children from their parents. In the conclusion to his book on risk, society and social work, Webb (2006) makes a nice case for basing social work on a sound ethical and value-based footing. Good judgement, he says, requires moral effort and a commitment to thinking.

What I'm trying to get at here is that in many situations, social workers are actually trying to answer the question 'What is the best course of action in this case?' To answer the question, the practitioner will certainly need to know all there is to know about the case. She will need to gather information and provide a full description of the situation. The descriptive data can then be analyzed and assessed. Based on the assessment a formulation can be made.

A case formulation should summarize, integrate and synthesize the knowledge brought together by the assessment process. It is out of this formulation that hypotheses emerge about the causes and character of the need, problem or concern. In turn, provisional hypotheses guide future observation and information gathering. In the light of new evidence and practice outcomes, hypotheses are under constant review, evaluation and revision.

Cognitive-behavioural and task-centred practices serve very well in these tasks. A deeper psychological understanding of the people in a case might be provided by a developmental attachment, relationship-based approach. Full social histories as well as rich behavioural descriptions of current relationships with partners, parents, children and professionals are invaluable. Assessments, analyses and formulations tell us what *is* the case.

We then need to decide what we *ought* to do and agree on the best course of action. Client and service user involvement is generally advised although there will be cases when other moral principles override values such as self-determination, collaboration and partnerships. Children at risk or a service user who might be a danger to himself or others might provide exceptions.

Knowledge of how personal psychologies and relationship dynamics might unfold and affect outcomes, particularly under conditions of stress, will need to be taken into consideration. Knowledge of attachment, relationship-based theory, cognitive-behavioural and social psychology help at such times. Developing a helping or therapeutic alliance with the service user is informed by person-centred, relationship-based and critically reflective approaches.

The best way forward

Let's return to me and my companion with what we fear might be her broken ankle on the remote mountainside. What's our best course of action?

We know lots of things. We have facts. We know what is the case. There is no reception on our mobile phone. Our knowledge of broken bones and first aid is rudimentary. My friend can't walk without heavy support. I'm not as young or as a strong as I used to be. It is late afternoon and the weather appears to be closing in. Our map tells us that half a mile further up the mountain, but getting further away from potential help, is a small ruin that may or may not have a roof for shelter. Two miles further down the track is a wood. It is seven miles back to the nearest village. If I seek help, it will be dark whatever time I return to my friend. We have a half litre of water and the remains of a fruit bar.

Do I leave my companion where she is, out in the open, and head back to the village? Do we struggle up the hill to the ruin and possible crude shelter before I go and then seek help? This will add at least an hour to the time before I can get back to the village. Do we go down the track to the wood in the hope there might be some protection from the impending rain and cold? Again, this will add time to the rescue. What ought we to do?

The facts of the case certainly encourage some decisions and discourage others. Nevertheless, the final course of action will have to be a judgement based on incomplete information. Of course, I will discuss what it is best to do with my injured friend. She will be party to the decision. But I know she doesn't like to make a fuss and tends to downplay her worries and needs. I'm not sure that her reassurance that she'll be fine staying where she is can be taken at face value. I know under pressure I tend to become more controlling but this might push both of us into more fixed views. As we weigh up the options, I notice that her forehead is beginning to sweat. The sky is also getting darker as the clouds thicken. In this tumble of facts, uncertainties, guesses and judgements, a decision must be made and action taken.

Best courses of action in social work are also taken on what is known about a case. However, information is rarely complete. There is uncertainty. Situations and circumstances constantly change.

The theories we use in social work help organize and explain the facts. They give practitioners and service users a sense of where they are so that they can take their bearings. So even if things change, at least they have a starting point. New events and information might change how the case is understood. A change in direction might be considered, based partly on relevant research-based evidence and partly on a re-assessment of the facts, people, interactions, aims and revised judgements.

Whether the judgement is quantitative or qualitative, the word 'best' is clearly evaluative. It seems reasonable to expect that social workers should be able to justify what they do. However, given the complex psychosocial nature of social work, the grounds of the justification, and therefore what is 'best practice' themselves have to be debated and argued. 'Critical best practice' social work captures much of this philosophy. This also takes us back to the book's opening chapter. Social workers are involved with the full rich, complex wonder of the human condition.

Practice therefore begins with observation, the collection of facts; the discussion of need; the negotiation of experience, beliefs, wants, plans, premises and relationships.

Based on the facts observed and collected, and the reality discussed and debated, an assessment and provisional formulation can be negotiated and agreed with the service user.

If the case is clear and the assessment sharp, the worker should look for research based evidence to support a course of action. The proposed course of action to be taken then needs to be described, explained and agreed with the service user. Social work of this kind might be seen as an applied, research-based, psychosocial science.

However, social work being what it is, there will be many cases, people and situations that don't lend themselves to a straightforward evidence-based practice. There might be no evidence-based research to inform the case. There might be too much uncertainty, ambiguity or instability in the situation to permit a clear way forward. The service user might be too indecisive, unpredictable, oppositional, suspicious or recalcitrant to co-operate with a worker-led solution. Or there might be cases where the need for care, compassion and contemplation, things that can't be met by technical, empirically based solutions, is what's wanted. Some service users simply value an encouraging word, a personal interest, a reliable visit, or a kind smile. In a culture of self-interest, believes Webb (2006), the defining strength of social work is its willingness to hold 'on to values of compassion, justice and caring . . .' (p 200)

In these cases, practices based on the relationship, reflexivity, constructive and critical best practices might be more suitable. These approaches are comfortable with the inherent uncertainty that characterizes practice with many service users. As well as drawing on the critical psychosocial sciences for their inspiration, there is also likely to be an interest in philosophy and the humanities.

In the sense that the hybrid approach being suggested here is based on both evidence and experience, science and the social work relationship, it might be described as 'pragmatic' (Trinder 2000).

In the sense that trial, error and interpretation are also involved, they might be described as 'heuristic'. Stephen Webb (2006: 129) helpfully explains this concept as he discusses the views of Katherine Tyson (1995). He notes her dismissal of social work based solely on experimentally-based evidence. She sees such evidence-based practices as narrow and over-simplified:

> against this tradition Tyson argues that research in social work is context-dependent and based on complex interpretative strategies or 'heuristics'. Practice research is more a process of inferential discovery based on trial and error rather than a mechanical instrument designed to prove observations. This perspective prioritises the immediate certainty of an intuitive and reflecting knowing for social work practitioners (Taylor and White 2000, Webb 2006: 130).

So, whereas social workers who use more formal theories and evidence-based approaches *deduce* what is going on and what must be done, critical, reflective and best practice approaches encourage social workers to *induce*, that is, draw out from the relationship with the service user what is thought to be going on and what might be done in practice. This inductive approach includes what service users have to say about their experience. It sees 'practice as a rich source of social work theory and knowledge that enhances or complements formal theories' (D'Cruz et al 2007: 74).

Pragmatic social work, and maybe critical best practice, faced with the realization that people and their lives are rarely simple, is happy both to deduce and induce, to make interventions backed by good research evidence but also to take actions that require judgements backed by sound values.

Keeping minds open

Throughout these pages we have met many theories and their associated practices. The variety and difference in their make-up reflects the subtlety, uncertainty and complexity of personal and social life. There is no consensus on how to make sense of these things. Psychology, sociology and political theory are rife with disagreement and debate about human nature and social order. Theories clash and there are fierce arguments between protagonists. This lack of consensus may be frustrating but the clashes reflect minds at work.

As an applied social science and human endeavour, social work has no choice but to echo these divides and debates. And having met so many diverse ideas there is always the danger of feeling bewildered.

But turn matters around, and the vast range of ideas about who we are and how we should live hints at the sheer exuberance that excites the study of sociology, psychology and social work. Remaining engaged with these subjects keeps the social work spirit alive.

The point of this advice is to urge practitioners to become intellectually engaged. We must be able to defend what we think and do while remaining open to new ideas and fresh research. People who have open minds are more inquisitive, appealing and adaptive. They remain enthusiastic about life.

Better knowledge and understanding tend to make most of us more articulate and authoritative. I may disagree with what you say but I shall respect your voice if it is clear, coherent and well-versed. Listening to you might even get me to change my mind.

Moreover, Secker (1993) found social work students who had reasonably clear ideas about theory and its uses also tended to be more open with their clients. They were also better listeners and generally more responsive. They used their theoretical ideas openly and as a shared guide with service users to find ways forward.

And still the wonder grew

The conclusion is, therefore, that social workers must remain questioning and critically reflective. They must be prepared to adapt, shift and change as they puzzle their way forward as best they can with those who use their services. They must be research literate and evidence-aware. If social workers, who, after all, work with people across the lifecourse in all states and all conditions, are to stay enthusiastic and committed, it is important that they never lose interest in all that the psychosocial sciences can throw at them.

With books, conferences and ideas on the one hand, and people, relationships and the muddled business of living on the other, it is entirely right and proper that social workers should continue to wrestle and struggle with the intellectual, emotional and moral demands of their job. We should have it no other way.

Bibliography

Adams, R. (2008) *Empowerment, Participation and Social Work* (4th ed.). Basingstoke: Palgrave Macmillan.

Ainsworth, M., Blehar, M., Waters, E, and Wall, S. (1978) *Patterns of Attachment: Psychological Study of the Strange Situation*. Hillsdale, NJ: Erlbaum.

Allen, J. G. and Fonagy, P. (Eds.) (2006) *Handbook of Mentalization-based Treatment*. Chichester: Wiley.

Appignanesi, L. (2008) All in the mind. *Guardian Saturday Review*, 16 February, pp 4–5.

Applegate, J. S. and Shapiro, J. R. (2005) *Neurobiology for Social Work: Theory and Practice*. New York: W.W. Norton.

Bandura, A. (1977) *Social Learning Theory*. Englewood Cliffs, NJ: Prentice Hall.

Bandura, A. (1997) *Self-Efficacy: The Exercise of Control*. New York: W. H. Freeman.

Bartlett, H. (1970) *The Common Base of Social Work Practice*. Washington: National Association of Social Workers.

Bauman, Z. (1992) *Intimations of Postmodernity*. London: Routledge.

Beck, A. T. and Emery, G. (1985) *Anxiety Disorders and Phobias: A Cognitive Perspective*. New York: Basic.

Beck, A., Freeman, A. and Associates (1990) *Cognitive Therapy of Personality Disorders*. New York: Guilford Press.

Beck, A. T., Rush, A. J., Shaw, B. F. and Emery, G. (1979). *Cognitive Therapy of Depression*. New York: Guilford Press.

Beck, A. T. and Weishaar, M. (1989) Cognitive therapy. In Freeman, A., Simon, K. M., Beutler, L. E. and Arkowitz, H. (Eds.) *Comprehensive Handbook of Cognitive Therapy*. New York Plenum, pp 21–36.

Beckett, C. (2006) *Essential Theory for Social Work Practice*. London: Sage.

Berger, P. L. and Luckmann, T. (1971) *The Social Construction of Reality*. Harmondsworth: Penguin.

Berlin, I. (1969) *Four Essays on Liberty*. Oxford: Oxford University Press.

Berlin, L. J., Ziv, Y., Amaya-Jackson, L. and Greenberg, M. T. (Eds.) (2005) *Enhancing Early Attachments*. New York: Guilford Press.

Bower, M. (Ed.) (2005a) *Psychoanalytic Theory for Social Work Practice: Thinking Under Fire*. London: Routledge.

Bower, M. (2005b) Psychoanalytic Theories for Social Work Practice. In Bower, M. (Ed.) *Psychoanalytic Theory for Social Work Practice: Thinking Under Fire*. London: Routledge, pp 3–14.

in Social Work: Critical Perspectives. Houndmills: Palgrave Macmillan, pp 15–37.

Fischer, J. (1978) *Effective Casework Practice*. New York: McGraw Hill.

Fook, J. (2002) *Social Work: Critical Theory and Practice*. London: Sage.

Fook, J. (2007) Reflective Practice and Critical Reflection. In Lishman, J., (Ed.) *Handbook for Practice Learning in Social Work and Social Care: Knowledge and Theory* (2nd ed.). London: Jessica Kingsley, pp 363–75.

Foucault, M. (1969) *Madness and Civilization: The Archaeology of Knowledge and the Discourse on Language*. New York: Harper.

Foucault, M. (1977) *Discipline and Punish: The Birth of the Prison*. Harmondsworth: Penguin.

Foucault, M. (1980) *Power/Knowledge: Selected Interviews and Other Writings 1972–1977*, C. Gordon (Ed.), Brighton: Harvester.

Freud, A. (1936) *The Ego and the Mechanisms of Defence*. London: Hogarth Press.

Garbarino, J. and Kostelny, K. (1993) Neighborhood and community influences on parenting. In Luster, L. T. and Okagaki, L. (Eds.) *Parenting: An Ecological Perspective*. Mahweh, NY: Lawrence Erlbaum Associates, pp 203–26.

Gerhardt, S. (2004) *Why Love Matters: How Affection Shapes a Baby's Brain*. London: Brunner-Routledge.

Germain, C. B. and Gittermain, A. (1996) *The Life Model of Social Work Practice: Advances in Theory and Practice* (2nd ed.). New York: Columbia University Press.

Giddens, A, (1990) *The Consequences of Modernity*. Cambridge: Polity Press.

Giddens, A. (1991) *Modernity and Self-identity*. Cambridge: Polity Press.

Goffman, E. (1961) *Asylums: Essays on the Social Situation of Mental Patients and Other Inmates*. Garden City, NY: Anchor.

Goffman, E. (1963) *Stigma: Notes on the Management of Spoiled Identity*. Englewood Cliffs, NJ: Prentice Hall.

Goldberg, S. (1999) *Attachment and Development*. London: Arnold.

Goldstein, H. (1973) *Social Work Practice: A Unitary Approach*. Columbia, SC: University of South Carolina Press.

Goldstein, H. (2002). The Literary and Moral Foundations of the Strengths Perspective. In Saleebey, D., (ed.) *The Strengths Perspective in Social work Practice* (3rd ed.). Boston: Allyn and Bacon, pp 23–47.

Gross, D. R. and Capuzzi, D. (2007) Helping Relationships: From Core Dimensions to Brief Approaches. In Capuzzi, D. and Gross, D.R., (Eds.) *Counseling and Psychotherapy* (4th ed.). Upper Saddle River, NJ: Pearson, pp 3–25

Habermas, J. (1968) *Knowledge and Human Interests*. London: Heinemann.

Hanmer, J. and Statham, D. (1999) *Women and Social Work: Towards a More Woman-centred Practice*. Basingstoke: Macmillan.

Hardiker, P. and Barker, M. (1991) Towards Social Theory for Social Work. In Lishman, J., (Ed.) *Handbook for Practice Learning in Social Work and Social Care: Knowledge and Theory* (2nd ed). London: Jessica Kingsley, pp 87–119.

Harris, J. (2008) State social work: constructing the present from moments in the past. *British Journal of Social Work*, 38, 662–79.

Hazler, R. J. (2007) Person-centred theory. In Capuzzi, D. and Gross, D. R. (Eds.) *Counseling and Psychotherapy* (4th ed.). Upper Saddle River, NJ: Pearson, pp 189–215.

Healy, K. (2005) *Social Work Theories in Context*. Basingstoke: Palgrave Macmillan.

Hebb, D. O. (1949) *The Organization of Behavior*. New York: Wiley.

Hennessey, R. (forthcoming) *Relationship Skills in Social Work Practice*. London: Sage.

Hollis, F. (1964) *Casework: A Psychosocial Therapy*. New York: Random House.

Hollis, F. (1972) *Casework: A Psychosocial Therapy* (2nd ed.). New York: Random House.

Holmes, R. (2008) *The Age of Wonder: How the Romantic Generation Discovered the Beauty and Terror of Science*. London: Harper Press.

Howe, D. (1993) *On Being a Client: Understanding the Process of Counselling and Psychotherapy*. London: Sage.

Howe, D. (1996) Surface and Depth in Social Work. In Parton, N. *Social Theory, Social Change and Social Work*. London: Routledge, pp 77–97.

Howe, D. (2005) *Child Abuse and Neglect: Attachment, Development and Intervention*, Basingstoke: Palgrave Macmillan.

Howe, D. (2008) *The Emotionally Intelligent Social Worker*, Basingstoke: Palgrave Macmillan.

Howe, D., Brandon, M., Hinings, D. and Schofield, G. (1999) *Attachment Theory, Child Development and Family Support: A Practice and Assessment Model*. Basingstoke: Palgrave Macmillan.

Hudson, B. and Macdonald, G. (1986) *Behavioural Social Work: An Introduction*. London: Macmillan.

Hume, D. (1739) *A Treatise of Human Nature*, ed. L. A. Selby-Bigge (1978), Oxford: Clarendon Press.

Illich, I. (1977) *Disabling Professions*. London: Marian Boyers.

Iveson, C. (2002) Solution-focused brief therapy. *Advances in Psychiatric Treatment*, 8: 149–57.

Jack, G. (1997) An ecological approach to social work with children and families. *Child and Family Social Work*, 2(2): 109–20.

Jack, G. (2000) Ecological influences on parenting and child development. *British Journal of Social Work*, 30: 703–20.

Jones, C. (1983) *State Social Work and the Working Class*. Basingstoke: Macmillan.

Perlman, H. H. (1957) *Social Casework: A Problem-solving Process.* Chicago: Chicago University Press.

Perlman, H. H. (1970) The Problem-solving Model in Social Casework. In Roberts, R. W. and Nee, R. H. (Eds.) *Theories of Social Casework.* Chicago: University of Chicago Press, pp 131–79.

Pincus, A. and Minahan, A. (1973) *Social Work Practice: Model and Method.* Itasca, IL: Peacock.

Pizzey, E. (1971) *Scream Quietly or the Neighbours Will Hear.* London: Penguin.

Plummer, K. (1995) *Telling Sexual Stories: Power, Change and Social Worlds.* London: Routledge.

Preskill, H. and Coghlan, A. T. (2003) *Using Appreciative Inquiry in Evaluation.* San Francisco: Jossey-Bass.

Rees, S. (1991) *Achieving Power.* Sydney: Allen and Unwin.

Reid, W. J. (2000) *The Task Planner: An Intervention Resource for Human Service Professionals.* New York: Columbia University Press.

Reid, W. J. and Epstein, L. (1972) *Task-centred Casework.* New York: Columbia University Press.

Reid, W. J. and Shyne, A. (1969) *Brief and Extended Casework.* New York: Columbia University Press.

Richmond, M. E. (1917) *Social Diagnosis.* New York: Free Press.

Rogers, C. R. (1942) *Counseling and Psychotherapy.* Boston: Houghton Mifflin.

Rogers, C. R. (1961) *On Becoming a Person.* Boston: Hougton Mifflin.

Rogers, C. R. (1986) Client-centred therapy. In Kutash, I. and Wolf, A. (Eds.) *Psychotherapist's Casebook: Theory and Technique in the Practice of Modern Therapies.* San Francisco: Jossey-Bass, pp 197–208.

Rose, N. (1999) *Governing the Soul: The Shaping of the Private Self* (2nd ed.). London: Free Association Books.

Ruch, G. (2005) Relationship-based practice and reflective practice: holistic approaches to contemporary child care social work. *Child and Family Social Work,* 10: 111–23.

Rymer, R. (1994) *Genie: A Scientific Tragedy.* New York: Harper Perennial.

Saleebey, D. (ed.) (1997) *The Strengths Perspective in Social work Practice* (2nd ed.). New York: Longman.

Saleebey, D. (2001) *Human Behavior and Social Environments: A Biopsychosocial Approach.* New York: Columbia University Press.

Saleebey, D. (2002) Introduction: Power in the People. In Saleebey, D. (ed.) *The Strengths Perspective in Social work Practice* (3rd ed.). Boston: Allyn and Bacon, pp 1–22.

Salzberger-Wittenberg, I. (1970) *Psycho-analytic Insight and Relationships: A Kleinian Approach.* London: Routledge and Kegan Paul.

Satir, V. (1967) *Conjoint Family Therapy.* Palo Alto, CA: Science and Behavior Books.

Schofield, G. and Beek, M. (2006) *Attachment Handbook for Foster Care and Adoption*. London: BAAF.

Schön, D. (1983) *The Reflective Practitioner: How Professionals Think in Action*. New York: Basic Books.

Secker, J. (1993) *From Theory to Practice in Social Work: The Development of Social Work Students' Practice*. Aldershot: Avebury.

Seed, P. (1973) *The Expansion of Social Work in Britain*. London: Routledge and Kegan Paul.

Seidman, S. (2004) *Contested Knowledge: Social Theory Today* (3rd ed.). Malden, MA: Blackwell.

Sheldon, B. (1982) *Behaviour Modification*. London: Tavistock.

Sheldon, B. (1998) Research and theory. In Cigno, K. and Bourn, D. (Eds.) *Cognitive-behavioural Social Work in Practice*. Aldershot: Ashgate Arena, pp 1–38.

Sheldon, B. and Macdonald, G. (2009). *A Textbook of Social Work*. London: Routledge Taylor and Francis.

Sheppard, M. (2006) *Social Work and Social Exclusion: The Idea of Practice*. Aldershot: Ashgate.

Sheppard, M. (2007) Assessment: from reflexivity to process knowledge. In J. Lishman (Ed.) *Handbook for Practice Learning in Social Work and Social Care*. London: Jessica Kingsley, pp 128–37.

Simon, B. (1994) *The Empowerment Tradition in American Social Work*. New York: Columbia University Press.

Siporin, M. (1975) *Introduction to Social Work Practice*. New York: Macmillan.

Skinner, B. F. (1971) *Beyond Freedom and Dignity*. Harmondsworth: Penguin.

Spartacus (2008) Beatrice Webb, retrieved on 6 February from: http://www.spartacus.school.net.co.uk/TUwebb.htm

Specht, H. and Vickery, A. (Eds.) (1977) *Integrating Social Work Methods*. London: Allen and Unwin.

Spitzer, S. (1975). Toward a Marxian theory of deviance. *Social Problems* 22(5): 638–51.

Statham, D. and Kearney, P. (2007) Models of Assessment. In Lishman, J. (Ed.) *Handbook for Practice Learning in Social Work and Social Care*. London: Jessica Kingsley, pp 101–14.

Susser, M. (1969) *Community Psychiatry: Epidemiologic and Social Themes*. New York: Random House.

Taleb, N. N. (2008) *The Black Swan: The Impact of the Highly Improbable*. London: Penguin.

Taylor, C. and White, S. (2000) *Practising Reflexivity in Health and Welfare*. Buckingham: Open University Press.

Taylor, C. and White, S. (2001) Knowledge, truth and reflexivity: the problem of judgement in social work. *Journal of Social Work*, 1(1): 37–59.

The International Association of Schools of Social Work and Federation of Social Workers (2001) Joint agreed definition 27 June, Copenhagen.

Thomas, E. J. (1970) Behavior Modification and Casework. In Roberts, R. and Nee, R. (Eds.) *Theories of Social Casework*. Chicago: University of Chicago Press, pp 181–218.

Thompson, S. and Thompson, N. (2008a) *The Critically Reflective Practitioner*. Basingstoke: Palgrave Macmillan.

Thompson, S. and Thompson, N. (2008b) Developing Critically Reflective Practice. *Wellbeing: The Quarterly Newsletter from Avenue Consulting Ltd. and Learning Curve Publishing*, 2(3), Wrexham: Avenue Consulting Ltd. Available from: www.well-being.org.uk

Thorndike, E. L. (1932) *The Fundamentals of Learning*. New York: Teachers College Bureau of Publications.

Trinder, L. (Ed.) (2000) *Evidence Based Practice: A Critical Appraisal*. Oxford: Blackwell Science.

Trower, P., Casey, A. and Dryden, W. (1988) *Cognitive-behavioural Counselling in Action*. London: Sage.

Truax, C. B. (1966) Reinforcement and Nonreinforcement in Rogerian Psychotherapy. *Journal of Abnormal Psychology*, 71: 1–9

Truax, C. B. and Carkhuff, R. R. (1967) *Towards Effective Counseling and Psychotherapy*. Chicago, IL: Aldine.

Tyson, K. (1995) *New Foundations for Scientific Social and Behavioral Research: The Heuristic Paradigm*. Englewood Cliffs: Prentice Hall.

von Bertalanffy, L. (1968) *General Systems Theory: Foundations, Development, Applications*. New York: George Braziller.

Wagner, P. (1994) *A Sociology of Modernity: Liberty and Discipline*. London: Routledge.

Walker, S. and Akister, J. (2005) *Applying Family Therapy*. Lyme Regis: Russell House.

Walter, J. L. and Peller, J. E. (1992) *Becoming Solution-focused in Brief Therapy*. New York: Bruner/Mazel.

Watson, J. B. and Raynor, R. (1920) Conditioned emotional reactions. *Journal of Experimental Psychology*, 3: 1–14.

Webb, S. A. (2006) *Social Work in a Risk Society: Social and Political Perspectives*. Basingstoke: Palgrave Macmillan.

Weick, A. C. and Chamberlain, R. (2002). In Saleebey, D. (ed.) *The Strengths Perspective in Social Work Practice* (3rd ed.). Boston: Allyn and Bacon, pp 95–105.

Weick, A. C., Rapp, P., Sullivan, W.P. and Kisthardt, W. (1989) A Strengths Perspective for Social Work Practice. *Social Work*, July, 34(4): 350–4.

Weiner, E. (2008) *The Geography of Bliss*. London: Black Swan.

White, J. (2008) Family Therapy. In Davies, M. (Ed.) *The Blackwell Companion to Social Work* (3rd ed.). Oxford: Blackwell, pp 175–83.

Whitney, J. (1937) *Elizabeth Fry: Quaker Heroine*. London: Geroge Harrop and Co.

Wilkinson, R. (2000) *Mind the Gap: Hierarchies, Health and Human Evolution*. London: Weidenfeld and Nicolson.

Wilson, K., Ruch, G., Lymbery, M. and Cooper, A. (2008) *Social Work: An Introduction to Contemporary Practice*. Harlow: Pearson Longman.

Winnicott, D. (1960) The Theory of the Parent-infant Relationship. In *The Maturational Process and the Facilitating Environment*. New York: International Universities Press, pp 37–55.

Witkin, S. (2002) Foreword. In Saleebey, D. (Ed.) *The Strengths Perspective in Social Work* (3rd ed.). Boston: Allyn and Bacon, pp xiii–xv.

Wolpe, J. (1990) *The Practice of Behavior Therapy* (4th ed.). New York: Pergamon.

Woodroofe, K. (1962) *From Charity to Social Work in England and the United States*. London: Routledge and Kegan Paul.

Young, A. F. and Ashton, E. T. (1956) *British Social Work in the Nineteenth Century*. London: Routledge and Kegan Paul.

Author Index

Subject Index

Printed in China